# Reset Your Inner Clock and Live Younger Longer

# RESET YOUR INNER CLOCK

*...and live younger longer!*

Roselyn Poon

RESET YOUR INNER CLOCK AND LIVE YOUNGER LONGER



Book cover by Bunker Hill Bradley

www.ResetYourInnerClock.com

Printed in the United States of America

First Printing: Aug 2019

ISBN: 9781733269803

# Dedication

**This book is dedicated to the 3 most wonderful gardeners a person could wish for, my mother Alice, my grandmother Nanna Poon and my soul mate, Bunker Bradley. It is thanks to their nurturing, support and love that I am the strong happy little human being I am today.**

**Bunker Bradley** – soul mate. Bunker is responsible for turning the light on and convincing me that I have a story that people should hear. Sometimes I get too involved with the mining of my thoughts to see the diamonds. It is then that Bunker helps me to rake through the mollusk heaps, and discover what I had too quickly discarded as unimportant. His creativity and tireless work ethic are only exceeded by his patience and love for me, which I am eternally grateful. He is also trying to teach me that I don't have to be perfect the first time around.

**Alice Poon** – mother. Mum is a boundless source of empowerment and love. She never judges me or uses her maternal power to dissuade me from some of my more dangerous adventures. Her ability to keep her loving spirit and enthusiasm for life burning bright through years of hardship and disappointment is inspiring. She has every right to be bitter and twisted but not so; she radiates warmth, compassion and love. She has shown me by her words and actions that celebrating life is the only way forward.

**Mary Poon** - Chinese grandmother. Nanna Poon was an amazing woman who in the early 1903's at the age of 22 traveled from China to Australia as a single mother with her two little boys aged 4 and 1. Her strong self-belief and survival instinct gave her the courage to go it alone with her boys. She never owned a house or accumulated wealth but she lived a fascinating life. During my visits she would give me wonderful advice on life and remind me that work will outlive me. Knowing that I come from a line of spiritually strong and courageous women helps me to quell the self-doubt that rises up on occasion, usually when I am not looking.

*The idea is to*

*die young as*

*late as possible.*

Ashley Montagu
Anthropoligist & Humanist

# Testimonials

As with anything in life, we have choices; we chose outcomes for our work, our play, our joy and happiness, our education, etc. How we enter into our later life is no different. Roselyn is living proof that we can chose to live younger for longer.
She has done a wonderful job of helping us to be aware that we do not have to age according to societal standards. She educates us on the environmental and society factors that affect our beliefs about aging and lays out an action plan to take control of our future. "Reset Your Inner Clock and Live Younger Longer" is a simple guide to taking control of your life, and changing the way we enter our later years.

Dr. Scott F Peterson
Health & Wellness Entrepreneur

Wow "Reset Your Inner Clock and Live Younger Longer" could change your life! It strikes at the heart of today's Wellness Movement. The timing is right on! Roselyn explains simply and convincingly how our "state of mind' directly affects our "state of being", our health and our longevity. It is a must read for everyone!

Bunker Bradley
Designer & Entrepreneur

This book is a must read for all ages. If you are 70, you want to be 50. If you're 50, you want to be 30. If you are 30, you want to be 20. In Roselyn's new insightful book "Rest Your Inner Clock and Live Younger Longer" she shows us how to do the "Time Warp" and get back 10 to 20 years of life by taking control of our mind and our life. Get motivated and get out there. Read this book and get your life back!
I love her Australian saying, "have a go", which means, "give it a try, you have nothing to lose". There are great examples throughout the book on how to fight the Premature Aging Virus, PAV and get your life back. We are never too old to learn new techniques and practices to stay younger longer. Roselyn gives us all the solid advice we need.

RJ DiDonato
International High-Tech Entrepreneur
Former President of the National Speakers Association L.A & Las Vegas

Roselyn cites the results of a study that suggests that positive age beliefs have been found to reduce stress and act as a positive influence for older individuals at high risk of dementia. If for no other reason, people should be reading this book!
The real benefit of Roselyn's book is the revelation of the Premature Aging Virus which she explains is responsible for robbing us of years of a wonderful productive and exciting future. She has a great quote in her book which says it all: "You don't think twice about protecting your computer from viruses, so how about transferring some of that love to your real personal computer-your mind."
Roselyn's comment about death is profound: "Death is a certainty, but you don't have to spend a third of your life going through OLD AGE to get there! You have a choice!"

Gary Doyle
Doyle Group

It is amazing how uplifting I felt while reading this book! It helped me remember that age is just a number and does not need to define a person at any stage of their life!
I appreciated Roselyn's references and workshop exercises that help reinforce how a powerful state of mind can create the courage to believe in the ability to "Be" and "Do" anything you choose! I also really appreciated her acknowledgement that her message may not be for everyone, however if they change their mind, they could always come back to it!

Linda Bakel
Marketing & Community Advocate

Everyone should read this book after they visited the plastic surgeon, they would then feel as young as they look!

Jim Brady
President, TPC Pacific Consulting

# Forward

"If I only knew then what I know now," the infamous phrase of life re-dos. What if I told you that your dreams can still become a reality and you can apply what you know now to now? Get ready to embark on a journey of self-discovery led by Roselyn Poon, narrated through her enchanting stories.

This book landed in my lap at a time in my life where I wasn't sure about how my next chapter would begin. In the few months following my mother's death, I crowned the new Mrs. Globe Classique, and stepped into a new role as a "former" beauty queen. My dermatologist informed me that I had skin cancer. Everything was spiraling. I was quickly sliding into the abyss of darkness and the Premature Ageing Virus quickly consumed my mindset. I was done. What else was there for me to do other than get old and allow the aging process to whittle me away to nothing. I fancy myself unique, but I'm willing to bet my story, or at least the arch of it, is familiar: life spirals and crashes, we whiter and age.

After reading and applying the exercises in Roselyn's book, my mindset began to shift. Her words rejuvenated me. This world is transcendent of the physical, my soul has needs. Awakened, not only did I regain my youthful outlook, but Roselyn's formula for second chances tapped into my most important asset, my belief in myself—my connection to my lived experience and innate wisdom, the things we are socialized against trusting.

Roselyn entertains us through her quick wit, and entertaining personal stories, but at the same time allows the reader to get in touch with the very impulses we have been trained against. Her message is centered on self and founded in the rediscovery of forsaken dreams leading to the founding of new habits of success making all dreams possible.

No matter where you are on your journey, I hope that you can connect with the ideas presented in this book and find a way to apply them to the fulfillment of your hopes and dreams. The waters of the Fountain of Youth are bubbling within you. Join Roselyn in *Reset Your Inner Clock*, and tap into your rejuvenating, healing, affirming spring of health and well-being. You'll thank yourself. You'll want to thank me, and we'll all thank Roselyn when we remove the impediments of aging and let our youth spring eternal.

With a smile,
Jeanette Lee
Mrs. Classique Globe 2018
High School Teacher: AP Literature and Composition

**Become a Foundation Member of Reset Your Inner Clock.**

**Go to RESETYOURINNERCLOCK.COM**

**and enter your name and email today.**

As we build our reference library you will receive further information on living younger longer, and as a member you will also receive early notification of our public events as they are scheduled.

# Table of Contents

***What am I selling?***

*A second chance.*

*The chance to take 10 – 20 years back and have it all – energy, time, wisdom, hindsight and the assets of your first go around.*

*A chance to achieve and experience things that you thought had passed you by.*

*The awareness that you can change your life time line and your future!*

# Introduction

## Naked and Afraid

This book is the culmination of 20 years of personal research, experimenting and refining the processes of living younger longer. My quest started in 1998 in a bay side suburb of Melbourne, Australia when I took a mind trip into old age and saw that it had nothing to offer me but misery.

I was the CEO and founder of a successful software company and I had just flown in from a tedious four-day business trip to Hong Kong. Even though I was tired and weary I drove straight to the office to catch up on what had happened during my four days away.

It was a Saturday and the office was empty. I turned on my PC and the first email was from a friend wishing me happy birthday. This was just what I needed, a reminder that another year had just disappeared. Now I was tired, stressed and miserable, so I jumped in the car and went birthday shopping.

Two hours later I was back at the office with a set of the latest electronic scales which could tell me what percentage of my body weight was fat. Right now, you are probably thinking that I was on some kind of suicide mission; what woman does this to herself on her 44th birthday? Good question.

The instruction booklet said that I had to stand naked on the scales to get a true reading so I locked the office door, turned off the lights, stripped off. What a surreal site it must have been; a room filled with computer screens emitting that eerie glow and, in the center, looking like an ancient Greek statue was a weary, over-weight, lily white, middle aged woman standing naked on a set of scales. To top it off I was trying to read the 4" x 4" instruction guide without my reading glasses. I covered my eyes with one hand, peeking through two fingers as I bent over to check out the reading. The scales had turned into the Dooms Day Machine! The reading glowed radioactive green as it flashed my body fat %. According to the body fat % table I was clinically dead or pretty close to it!

I knelt down putting my hands on my knees feeling thoroughly beaten and defeated. I didn't even have the energy or will to cry. All I could hear was the catching of my breath. How did this happen? My last conscious memory was of being somewhere in my 30's, young, excited, looking to the future with hope, and so many great plans. It isn't fare, somewhere along the way I had lost sight of time. Head down, bum up as we say in Australia, working hard to get ahead; get ahead of what? The last few years had been particularly brutal business wise and personally, and now this little electronic gadget confirmed my worst fears. The end was in site. I can feel the pain and the hopelessness even now as I remember that moment on the scales.

I don't know how long I stood there crunched over in a daze, trying to make sense of what was left of my life when suddenly I had an epiphany. Out of the blue, I wondered what my life looked like through the eyes of a thirty-two-year-old. I have no idea why I picked 32. The air filled with static electricity, as I stood up and slowly looked around the office taking stock of my life from the view point of a younger me, a 32-year-old me.

The office looked the same as it had minutes earlier but my experience of it changed dramatically. I now saw that I had a successful software company with a long list of blue-chip clients, a sexy black Porsche convertible in the parking lot, a wonderful house in the fashionable part of town, all my fingers and toes, no emotional baggage, respect from my fellow Porsche racing drivers, and at least thirty years to grow the business into a multi-million-dollar corporation. This is a pretty cool life for someone who is only thirty-two. Retirement and old age didn't even rate a mention!

Wow, what a difference a couple of minutes can make! I was now standing taller on the scales when it dawned on me that no one had the right to tell me when I was old or past my use by date, let alone some lifeless electronic gadget that had seduced my subconscious. There and then I knew that I had to take full responsibility for my aging and life timeline.

How could it be this easy? The answer is simple. I had looked into the future and it was sad, dark, lonely and decidedly short on cash. The misery that overcame me was sufficient to create a big enough why to change, and in the process, I had discovered the key. The trick was I had to work out how to permanently reset my inner clock to that thirty-two-year-old Roselyn. I had experienced the change in my state of mind, which in turn instantly changed my future as you can't have one without the other, however I had to find out how to make this a true transformation and not just a blip on my timeline.

I had stepped on the Dooms Day Machine a tired old middle-aged mess looking down the barrel of a miserable retirement, and minutes later I jumped off a happy, invigorated and excited young woman who had found the key to change her life now and the future. Youthful enthusiasm, wisdom, experience, not to mention the shiny black Porsche and more than 30 years to go to make my millions was now mine. I kicked the Dooms Day Machine to the curb, got dressed and took the rest of the week-end off.

I left the office feeling inspired and motivated to quickly learn as much as I could about how to solidify this youthful state of being. I needed to learn how to permanently reprogram my brain and reframe my thinking so that my body and spirit would be congruent. I immediately set about researching anti-aging, living healthier and the science of reprogramming my brain.

Resetting my inner clock was life changing, and over the years I have developed an understanding of what had happened during my life up until that fateful Saturday afternoon. I had been living under the influence of what I have termed the Premature Aging Virus (PAV). This is a societal problem where the media, government, community, friends and family actively work at programming you to be what they feel is stereotypical for your age and theirs. This was a toxic situation and required a cure ASAP.

In brief, the cure for the PAV is a healthy mix of updating your beliefs, creating compelling reasons and visions to live younger longer, simplified Neuro Linguistic Programming (NLP) processes, Kaizen and the latest and greatest, Neuroscience. NLP has been around since the early seventies and is a very effective tool for reframing your state of mind and your experience of the world around you. Over the past decade I have studied and implemented many beneficial mindset changes using NLP. The most impactful change is the knowing that I will live to celebrate my one hundred and twentieth birthday, and there will not be a set of body fat scales in sight!

Over the last few years neuroscientists have published many papers and books on the advances in brain research and introduced us to neuroplasticity. The first official Neuroscience scientific event was as recent as 2001. It is an exciting era to be alive as scientists continue to uncover the mysteries of our biology and our brain. Combining mainstream neuroscience with NLP and the power of belief gives you a dynamic set of tools and processes to reprogram your thinking and state of mind, starting with your inner body clock. What good is the desire for change without the time needed to implement it and reap the rewards?

Since that day in my office I have remained true to my new inner clock and it is common place for people to think that I am a great deal younger than my driver's license. In my reality I am in my early forties with an expected life span of another exciting youthful sixty to eighty years.

Resetting my inner clock has rewarded me in so many areas of my life that to list them all is a book in itself. One of the immediate benefits of resetting my inner clock was stress reduction. I no longer worry about retirement and having enough money to see me through the twilight years. My revived enthusiasm for life supercharged my income earning capability. I am a ball of energy glowing with possibilities, and everyone wants to work with me and have me on their team. I provide an unusual combination of youthful energy and years of experience spiced with a tad of wisdom.

There were a few surprises when I first reset my inner clock, for example I did not expect it to have an impact on how my mates and I related to each other. In the early years I did not notice much of a difference, however over time the gap has widened. It makes sense, as they are looking at the world through the eyes of someone getting ready for retirement, and I am in the fledgling years of my second life time and new career.

I want you to understand what ages you prematurely and how you can reset your inner clock to get back that lost time. You do want another crack at the past ten years, don't you? Just think what life would be like if you had another 10 – 20 years inserted into your life now. How would tomorrow and the next day look? How would you feel? Could you start breathing again? Could you treat the economic down turn as a blip on your timeline and regroup?

When I realized that time had run over me and I had very little to show for it, I was angry with the world, myself, and life. It just didn't seem fair. I wanted that time back or at least the past ten years so I could have a second crack at it with hind sight and wisdom.

I want you to have that hind sight and wisdom too. You picked this book up so you must be at least wondering about your life and future. Stop thinking and commit to doing something now. Reset your inner clock, create your visions and living younger mindset and use the tools in this book to create an exciting future.

Remember this toxic premature aging virus can be overcome. At this point in time you have choices. Let's face it, we are all going to age and die sooner or later. The million-dollar questions are how will you age and when will it all end? This is your chance to have some input into at least the how and maybe even the when, give or take a decade. It is your choice. Chose to stand up and go into the future swinging (punches that is) or admit defeat and spend half of your life time in old age.

Thanks to our modern living conditions and medical breakthroughs our mortality rate is extending each year. On the surface it sounds pretty good but what are you going to do with that extra time at the end? Are you going to spend more of your life time living old, or are you going to shake it up now so that when you are on the tail end you are still living life and not just waiting to clock out?

It is not too late. Join me and millions of others around the world in our quest to live younger longer by creating the right state of mind and beliefs to carry us through this life time with energy and intention. The anti-aging longevity lifestyle is not a two-week wonder drug. It needs a solid commitment which in turn needs a big enough why and a mindset geared up for the long haul.

I know what is involved in changing. I have over 35 years of experience in change management centered on the study of human behaviors, intentions and mind sets in the corporate environment. I have learned that we humans are not always perfect and that our emotions, wants, focus, goals and willpower are like little boats on the ocean; always moving, sometimes gently with the breeze and other times rocking and reeling as waves come crashing down upon us. Appreciate the days when you skim across the water laughing and enjoying the ride and know that when the waves start crashing down on you and exhaustion sets in that this is just a moment in time. Go with the storm. The worst thing you can do is fill your mind with doubt and negative self-talk. Self-doubt is a toxic acid that quickly dissolves your self-esteem and spirit until there is nothing left but that hollow feeling in your stomach called defeat. It is with this understanding of human nature that I have written this book, and it is my wish for you that you work your way through the coming pages and create your younger more youthful you.

This book is primarily about making you aware of the Premature Aging Virus™ that has been stealing years from your life and what you need to do to fight back. I know not everyone has the time and inclination to read through piles of research papers and books but that doesn't mean you should be excluded from the benefits of life changing scientific research. I have done the reading and the research for you and distilled it down to a few straight forward steps and processes.

Each chapter explains the concept, gives you some examples and in most instances provides you with exercises for you to have a go. I am a great believer that doing is the best form of learning.

Start now by feeling great about yourself for being smart enough to take the option that the ninety-year-old you would want you to take.

Step into chapter one with the intention of resetting your inner clock, taking control over the rest of your life and creating a more hopeful future for yourself and those around you.

You are not alone, join the Reset Your Inner Clock community and become a Life Olympian.

Now, get cracking!

Most people are aware that there are hundreds of books and websites with information that will help them delay the aging process however, they chose not to read them or follow the advice as this would mean they had to confront their fears about aging. In other-words old age is considered less of an issue than confronting it and knowing that you can do something about it. Excusing yourself for aging prematurely due to lack of information seems preferable to sustaining youth. Why? Is it because by confronting premature aging and trying to do something about it, you are taking responsibility for your aging, whereas ignorance means that you are just one of the masses and growing old is just how it is?

Roselyn

# Chapter 1

## The Premature Aging Virus

*Kill the PAV before it prematurely kills you.*

The PAV is a nasty psychological mixture of toxic and outdated beliefs regarding aging, combined with a gross misunderstanding of the importance time has on your aging.

Sadly, the PAV is a silent killer of valuable youthful life through its subconscious power to make us feel, and consequently be older than we need to be. It is a powerbroker in your subconscious which in turns drives your state of mind and being. Simply put, if you believe you are old you will be old. A neat little downward spiral. If you believe you are younger you will live younger; this is the upward spiral we are aiming for.

Let's start by looking at the literal meaning of the words which make up the Premature Aging Virus.

- Premature:
  - Mature or ripe before the proper time.
  - Happening, arriving, existing or performed before the proper time.
  - Arriving or received without due authentication or evidence.
  - Uncommonly early.
- Aging:
  - The organic process of growing older and showing the effects of increasing age.
- Virus:
  - Contagious or poisonous matter.
  - The causative agent of a disease.
  - Any morbid corrupting quality in intellectual or moral conditions; something that poisons the mind or the soul.

** Webster's on-line Dictionary and WordNet Dictionary.*

Sounds nasty doesn't it? And well it should because it is robbing you of years of a wonderful productive and exciting future.

The PAV starts at birth and grows quietly for many years, until one day someone or something triggers the thought in your mind that you aren't as young as you used to be. This tragic event acts like a switch turning the once dormant PAV into an active participant in your mind's eye and decision making.

The moment before the PAV was turned on, you would have thought your aching shoulder was due to over extending in the kitchen or the gym, but now the PAV has you thinking that it is probably the first signs of old age.

We humans in general, believe what we see and hear around us. If our friends are attributing their aches and memory losses to old age then so will we. Whereas time has nothing to do with it. Our body just needs some TLC. It is asking us to change our lifestyle and habits. The problem of course is if we don't put it down to old age, we have to do something about it and that means getting involved with our body and mind.

The PAV goes undetected because it is psychological. It is a group of beliefs you have on old age and aging which you have developed over the years based on your environment. Environment includes people, places, activities, media, and education, everything you have ever come in contact with.

*The PAV is just one of a number of psychological powerbrokers that govern your experience of your world, however it is the only one we are concerned with in this book because it is the one that controls your life time line. .... Roselyn Poon*

## Toxic Beliefs About Aging and Misunderstanding Time are the Basis of the Pav

### Let's look at time first

You need to understand what time is and how it affects you. Time is a form of measurement in the same way that inches, kilometers, kilograms and ounces are forms of measurement. Time makes it easier for us to plan events and interact with the rest of the world. Time is just like inches on a ruler or page numbers in a book, and has no magical powers in and of itself.

*Time does not age you.*

You age because your biology deteriorates not because you have been around for 40, 50, 60 years.

According to bio-science your body progressively slows down new cell reproduction, and speeds up the rate of dying cells from the day you are born. The speed depends on the individual and it can be positively and negatively impacted by your life style.

I have met people who are in their early 30's and because of their love of the sun they look like they have been baking for 60 years. Think about some of the people you have met over the years.

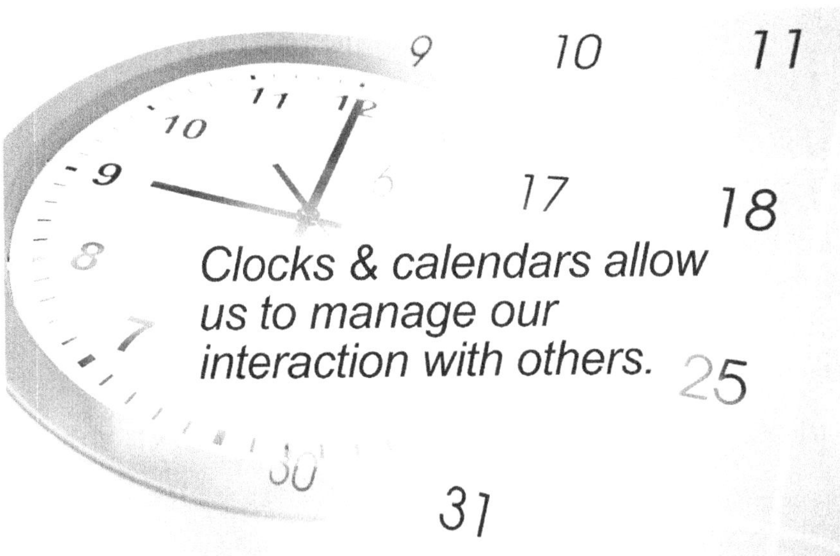


The key point is that you shouldn't blame your hearing problems or aching bones on time. Time has nothing to do with it, which is why you can step away from time and have real input into your aging and future.

Just as I said earlier, think of age like a page number in a book. The page number is simply a way of noting when something happened. The page number has no bearing on the plot or the characters.

Personally, my biography is up to page 66, however my character as described on page 66 is a 45-year-old serial entrepreneur. What does your biography look like?

*Once you become an adult time no longer has any bearing on who you are... Roselyn Poon*

Albert Einstein had a great deal to say about time, and it was he who made me realize that time is a human construct.

The other key characteristic of living younger longer is understanding the power of your beliefs, and I don't mean your religious spiritual beliefs, although they are very important. I am talking about your everyday understanding of life around you and how you fit in.

**Now the elephant in the room – your beliefs**

Repeated toxic thoughts about aging eventually become toxic beliefs, and when you combine this mind set with your environment, you unknowingly feed the Premature Aging Virus.

Understanding how beliefs work is fundamental to understanding the PAV.

A belief is the result of a thought that has repeatedly run through your mind to the extent that it is now part of your subconscious. Once it is installed into your subconscious it runs on auto-pilot.
Beliefs can be good, bad or otherwise and they can change.

A thought is in your conscious mind. You are consciously thinking of things all the time, e.g. wonder what the weather will be today, will the traffic be bad this morning, what are we going to do for dinner tonight? You can see it, evaluate it, process it and dismiss it.

Thoughts are transient and occur constantly throughout your day. However, thoughts you have that express your genuine feelings about something important to you are very likely to become beliefs if they cross your mind frequently enough. They will ultimately create an imprint on your subconscious.

Case in point is my fear of contracting cancer. I can remember being concerned about it as early as my mid-teens when my father was diagnosed with bowl cancer. There is always a starter trigger to a belief. Consequently, I became consciously aware of anything in the news or the press which talked about possible triggers for cancer.

My preoccupation with consciously avoiding anything which was even vaguely thought to be carcinogenic meant that ultimately, I avoided these environments and things without even thinking about it. I was never attracted to a guy who smoked or clubs that allowed smoking. I was not interested in sunbathing on the beautiful Australian beaches. These actions or non-actions were a direct result of my core belief about cancer.

Eventually, a repeated thought be it good or bad, will become stored in your subconscious and become automatic.

*"As a man thinketh in his heart so is he," not only embraces the whole of a man's being but is so comprehensive as to reach out to every condition and circumstance of his life. A man is literally what he thinks, his character being the complete sum of all his thoughts.*

*Author, James Allen 1864 - 1912*

When something becomes a belief, it becomes part of your subconscious mind. It becomes automatic. A belief has an incredible effect on your feelings, actions and thoughts. A lot of the time this occurs without you being aware of it.

Think about driving to the office or a friend's home. The first few times you consciously looked for the right roads and registered landmarks of interest along the way. Over a period of time you are able to drive there on automatic. Key landmarks have faded into obscurity. Eventually you don't even see what is actually there. You are no longer traveling through reality. You are experiencing a partial mind trip. Just like driving itself is eventually handled by your subconscious.

Think about the times when you have done something only to wonder if you actually did it. I sometimes have this issue with our garage door. It is so automatic to hit the remote to close it that I do it totally unconsciously and on occasion I think to myself, 'did I close the garage door?' I have no conscious memory of doing it, so I turn around and drive home to make sure. So far, I have closed it every time, but I am sure I will always return home to check.

Your subconscious makes it possible to live the way you do. It handles all that repetitive stuff, so be mindful of the 'stuff' you actively or accidently feed your subconscious.

The gist of it is that your environment feeds your subconscious every second of your waking life. In the majority of cases this happens without you being remotely aware or concerned, as you and your conscious self gets on with everyday life. The sad fact is that while you are busy living life, your subconscious is unfettered, busily sucking-up information from your surroundings, translating it into neuron speak and storing these interpretations for possible use at a later date.

---

*BTW: Our unconscious mind is capable of processing in excess of 11,000,000 bits of information per second as compared to our conscious mind which is pushing it to process 16 – 50 bits per second. Just this fact alone is enough to give you a nose bleed. Right now, you are wondering how on earth can you vet this amount of information your unconscious is sucking up and continue to have brain power left to eat and breath. True, this is an impossible task if it is as black and white as the figures make it seem, however fortunately for you and me the solution is in the detail.*

---

The Premature Aging Virus is insidious and similar to a computer virus that infects your personal computer. We have all been on the wrong end of a computer virus, and know full well the devastation it can wrought on our computers.

Generally, the computer virus infects our computer without us being aware at the time. It is nearly impossible to know how, where or when the virus first attached itself to our computer.

There are an infinite number of computer viruses in cyber space, just waiting to hook into our poor unsuspecting computer, and each virus acts out in its own way. All we know is that over time our computer starts to run slower, files are corrupted, strange blue screens pop up and eventually our computer crashes and burns. At some point in time we realize what is going on, and run a virus detector or bring in a technical guy to do it for us. The net result varies from no harm done, to losing everything and having to start again.

The PAV is the 'human' virus infecting our subconscious, and it behaves in a very similar way to the computer virus on our computer.

You have a choice. You can live with the PAV until the end of the line, accepting your aches, pains and general feelings of old age as normal, or you can run a PAV virus detector on your subconscious and recover some of your lost years before it is too late.

*You don't think twice about protecting your computer so how about transferring some of that love and attention to your real personal computer, your mind....... Roselyn*

Time to find out what is going
on in your subconscious.

# Chapter 2

## How You Contracted the Premature Aging Virus (PAV)

*The PAV is the result of a lifetime of propaganda about aging & time ...... Roselyn*

### How I discovered the PAV?

It was the day of my 45th birthday when I realized what was going on. Prior to that time, I was unaware of the PAV and the impact it was having on my life. Everyone around me seemed to be going through the same experiences, albeit some more successfully than others. It wasn't until I had an epiphany on my 45th birthday that I realized I had been living on autopilot most of my life.

*Personal story: **(The full story is covered in the Naked and Afraid section at the start of this book.)***

*I was a tired, stressed, overweight mid-forties woman heading for a miserable cash strapped retirement. It was a Saturday and I was alone in the office feeling disgusted with how I had worked so hard and not really reached my goals, and to make matters worse, it was looking like I never would.*

*My thoughts were simple, I was nearly 50 and 50 is nearly 60 when suddenly I experienced an epiphany. I asked myself how my life and future would look and feel through the eyes of someone who was 32 rather than 45.*

*The insight was life changing. Nothing had physically changed and yet everything had changed. My world through the eyes of a young 32-year-old woman was inspiring. Instead of feeling overwhelmed by the feeling that I was running out of time, I felt inspired and energized. I had at least 30 years to grow my business and turn my finances around. The best part was that unlike the first time I was 32 with a lot to learn, this time I had 12 years of experience and hindsight to begin with...... Roselyn*

The epiphany showed me that my world was not so bad, and that I just had to experience it through a younger state of mind.

The next realization was that there was no law saying I had to be age 45 as society deemed. I could be any age I wanted, within reason of course, so I chose an age that I was immediately comfortable with, age 32.

It sounds unbelievable but within a couple of minutes the stress of pending retirement and all that it meant was gone. I stepped on those fat scales in despair, and hopped off energized and full of life. I am not spinning you a line. It really happened and it can happen to you too.

Upon further reflection and analysis, I realized that I had been going through life like a passenger on a train. Never questioning my direction or speed. I had to give this train a name so I could have something to fight against so I called it the Old Age Express.

Life seems hectic enough without stopping and taking extra time to think about it. It is so much easier to focus on the daily grind of the squeaky wheel than question the larger things in life. Meanwhile your unconscious self is hanging around your environment picking up on everything. It is quietly ensuring that you are aging in accordance with your social norm. Meaning, if your 50$^{th}$ birthday signifies the start of the end in your group of friends then that is how you will start thinking about your life.

*BTW: Inevitably you will start making decisions with the view that you are no longer on a growth path but a retirement path. ... Roselyn*

Once I became aware of the PAV I was armed and ready to fight for my life and my future.

I am now age 45 having spent 65 years on this Earth and retirement has been pushed so far into the future that it may never come.

---

*Personal story: I pushed the emergency stop button on the Old Age Express over twenty years ago and jumped off. It was a life-saving event for me and now you are learning how to save the rest of your life... Roselyn*

---

Becoming aware of your personal beliefs on aging is at the core of taking control of the rest of your life.

Now that you know the PAV is a group of toxic beliefs about aging that prematurely robs you of valuable living younger years, you probably want to go straight to the cure however, you first need to understand how it started, and how it grew to be so powerful. This understanding is invaluable in helping you to successfully eradicate it from your life.

**So, let's start at the beginning.**

## The Generic Life Journey on The Old Age Express

Our environment and societal norms have an enormous impact on the growth of the PAV, and help to keep it burning bright.

All societies and cultures have their own social constructs, ethics, standards of behavior, and lifetime maps. I was born and continue to live in a western society, so my personal examples are based on this society, however the general process is the same for any society, it is the detail that varies; e.g. schooling happens in most societies however the school years and how and what is taught varies from one group to another. Another example of a process that happens globally is the union of two people. The acceptable protocol and ceremonies vary from one country or society to the next but the event is the same, two people committing to each other.

I like to think of the accepted normal life's journey as a train ride on the Old Age Express.

We board an Old Age Express train on the day we are born. It takes us through life, stopping or passing through ages and life events like stations on a railway line.

It doesn't take long for the rhythmic sound of the train and the gentle rocking motion to dull our senses. We are surrounded by our family and friends, and like passengers on a real train we settle in and leave the speed and route up to the driver.

---

**A Generic Life Journey:** Born, pre-school at 4, elementary school at 5, high school at 12, college at 17, adulthood at 21, family and career through to 50, middle aged at 50, retirement at 65, old age at 68 and death at 80.

---

Whose life is this? Is it yours? Maybe the ages and actual events are not exactly as described, but it is not too far from what has been pre-loaded into your subconscious and re-enforced throughout your life. This generic life journey and its associated roles have been the basis for most of your decision making since the day you were born.

*BTW: You didn't even audition for this life journey. Your starring role came freely loaded into your subconscious. Sadly, like software that comes preloaded with your PC, it is easier to use it than to question its relevance to your needs. .... Roselyn Poon*

In all seriousness, your Old Age Express train and your life time line were pretty much in place before you were born. Your parents and the environment you were born into is responsible for getting you onto your first Old Age Express. From that point it was just a matter of you going along with it, and becoming another compliant unaware passenger. Your train is filled with people and places that have been together for a long time, and this makes for a safe and secure ride.

A typical Old Age Express train ride for someone born in western society during the 50's and 60's goes something like this (the station numbers represent your chronological age):

**Generic Western Society Train Line – trains departing every second.**

- Station 4 – pre-school
- Station 5 – primary school
- Stations 11 – 14 - junior high school
- Stations 15 – 17 – senior high school, college or working
- Stations 18 – 20 - university or working
- Stations 21 – 30 - start career, marriage, family
- Stations 31 – 40 - career peaks, family matures
- Stations 41 – 50 - career slow down, family spreads
- Stations 51 – 65 – career growth stops, move towards redundancy and retirement
- Stations 66 – 85 – retired, old age, end of the line

Maybe the ages and the actual events are not exactly yours, but it is not far away from what we have been programmed from birth. This is the generic life journey most of us are familiar with.

Obviously, there are thousands of variations to this life time line but the key stations are pretty much a constant. Take a good look at it. You spend your first twenty years getting to be an adult, you then get to spend only twenty years in full flight as an adult and then you spend the remaining 45 years on the way out. Does this seem fair to you? It doesn't look good to me.

There are certain stages in your early years that make good sense to stay on the train, however by the time you are in your twenties you could potentially jump off the train and take control of your life time line and aging.

Following is my actual train ride until I got off at Station 45 and never returned. The station number represents my chronological age.

**My Train Line – Departed Warracknabeal Hospital, April 1, 1953 at 6:15am**

- Stations 1 - 4 – lived with my parents and Chinese grandmother in a variety of low income inner suburban flats (apartments)
- Stations 4 - 7 – attended many inner suburban primary schools
- Station 8 – settled into our first home and went to local primary school
- Stations 11 – 16 attended local public high school (in Australia we go to high school for 6 years – there is no junior and senior split)
- Stations 17 – 18 college studying IT (originally referred to as Computer Studies, there was no IT university course at this time)
- Stations 19 – 26 started IT career, married, built first home, started free-lance software development
- Station 27 - divorced, started own IT company Computer Link

- Station 32 – purchased first Porsche, IT company growing
- Station 36 – purchased second Porsche, IT company still growing
- Station 40 – purchased Porsche race car, IT company still going strong
- Stations 41 – 43 Racing-driver in Porsche Cup Race Series, IT company took a hit from global economic recession.
- Station 45 - Life changing epiphany – jumped off the Old Age Express.

As you can see, I only listed key events that had a pretty solid impact on my journey; however, note that I did not get off the train until Station 45. I moved from one carriage to the next, changed seats, met new fellow travelers but it never occurred to me to get off the train until Station 45.

If you have not yet reached conventional middle age please stay with us. You are one of the lucky ones who can make an impact much earlier in your life's journey. For the most part I will assume that you are chronologically 45 - 65 and living in the western world. Growing up in Asia and in the East is somewhat different, however the train concept still prevails.

The impact of the Premature Aging Virus™ increases intensity around middle age, sometimes earlier depending on your environment and your lifestyle.

## Factors That Impact Your Pav

### Your date of birth

The date of your birth and the environment you were born into have a massive impact on your life journey, and you had no say in either. You board your first train based on your parents' life journey thus far. Even if you were given up as a baby for adoption, this event was caused by your biological parents' life journey and the train they were on at the time of your birth.

Following is a simple demonstration of the impact your date of birth can have on your life journey. In Australia a child must be 5 years of age by May 1st in the year that they start school, not kindergarten. This means some children will start up to a year later than their friends by virtue of their birth date. Through no fault of your own the day you were born dictates which train you will board.

*BTW: Unfortunately, I have heard that generally society sees the children who started school at 4+ years to be smarter than the ones who had to wait until they were 5+.*

In the early part of your life journey you have no input or control over the train you are on. You don't know what stations lay ahead, where it is going or when it is going to stop. You are a compliant little passenger.

**Your childhood environment**

Where you live also has a great impact on your formative years principally because it influences which schools you can attend, which in turn affects the environmental messages absorbed by your sub-conscious and colors your initial view of the world and your self-esteem.

Your childhood environment including family and friends contribute greatly to your state of mind and self-perception during these formative years. Add to this, beliefs and points of view actively taught to you by your teachers, family, and role models.

As a child these are some of the main sources of input to your beliefs about yourself and your world.

**Your teenage environment**

Around your late teens you're either still studying, working, travelling or unemployed. A person studying will be surrounded by a very different environment to one who is working, travelling or unemployed. It is at this stage in your life that you are equipped to start making your own decisions about your environment and socialization, however bear in mind that your choices are heavily influenced by your life journey thus far.

Often people will not vary too far from their predetermined life script, and stay on the train comfortable in their surroundings.

Most people travel the path of least resistance and leave the direction and speed up to the train driver. Other passengers are too busy having fun on the train to worry about the speed or direction. Only a few take the controls early on.

**Your adult environment**

During the remainder of your life you will have continual influences from your childhood associations and many new inputs from your work places, travel, research, adult interests etc.

These influences apply to every part of your development including your attitude towards aging, and it is this set of beliefs that we are concerned with in this book.

Over the years your beliefs about aging and subsequent death have developed probably without you being aware of it. Maybe close relatives have passed away round the same age as each other. This age and associated demise have not gone unnoticed by your subconscious. The events have quietly slipped into your subconscious setting up the idea that your train journey through life will end around the same age.

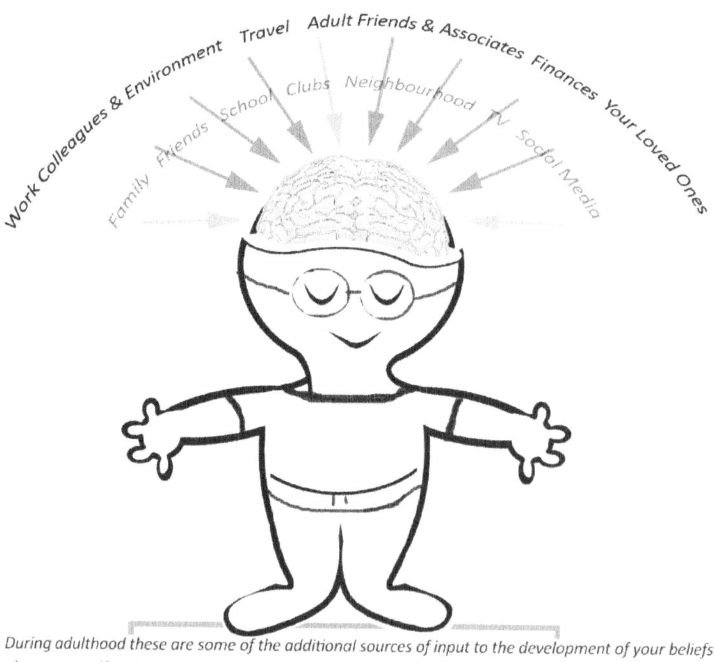

*During adulthood these are some of the additional sources of input to the development of your beliefs about your self and your life.*

The truth of the matter is you are unconsciously setting up a self-fulfilling prophecy.

*"The mind is everything. What you think you become." ........ Buddha 563BC – 483 BC*

The PAV is your set of beliefs on aging, and where you believe you are in your life time-line. These beliefs affect your decision making and your experience of the world. The PAV is fed by your surroundings, family, friends, the media, government, insurance companies, banks, in short, everything you come in contact with.

To demonstrate how your environment has the power to affect your thinking I am going to employ the assistance of a couple of fictitious characters. Please note these are not real people and if your name happens to be Tom, Fred or Doris please accept my apologies as it is strictly accidental.

Story: Fred and Doris are constantly talking about what they are going to do when they retire, even though they have ten years to go. They are looking forward to retirement and start planning and making financial and lifestyle decisions based on their pending retirement. They have a set of beliefs that define retirement as a wonderful happy time in their lives.

Their close friend Tom supports them in their planning but he is thinking that retirement is not for him. He is happy with the here and now. Tom's conscious self has not been listening too intently to his friends but his unconscious hasn't missed a syllable.

The unfortunate situation is that Tom's unconscious has picked up on Fred and Doris's enthusiasm for retirement, and this has started Tom wondering about retirement. Their enthusiasm triggers Tom's PAV and before he knows it, he is checking the prices of Winnebago's on E-bay.

This in and of itself is not a problem. It is Tom's beliefs about what retirement means that has a potentially negative outcome.

Tom believes that retirement is the beginning of the end. He associates retirement with slowing down, becoming less productive and old age. Therefore, because he has started wondering about retirement, and he believes retirement signifies old age, he starts to believe that he is moving into old age. Tom's new belief that he is moving into the old age phase of his life starts to influence his conscious thoughts to match his internal representation of getting older and retiring.

One of the saddest outcomes of this is that prior to all this happening Tom had a lifelong passion to go to Egypt, and volunteer on an archeological dig, but now he is starting to feel that it is too late. He is thinking that maybe Egypt was just a pipe dream and it goes on the 'could've, would've, had I only' list.

The insidious PAV kicks in big time as Tom starts to feel that he has let himself down by waiting too long to follow his dream. Tom begins to diminish in his own eyes, his self-esteem is weakened a little and the aging process speeds up to maintain congruency between his mind and body.

Tom was once a happy fifty-year old and over the past few months due to influences he was not even consciously aware of, he started to age in accordance with his surroundings.

---

Scary isn't it? Can you see how people and events surrounding you have at times influenced your opinions and then your beliefs? The PAV is insidious and works like a virus which attacks your computer and crashes your system. It is not until your computer comes to a grinding halt, that you start to wonder what happened, and set about virus protecting your computer.

## Environmental factors that feed the pav

At the time of writing this book there are over three hundred million people in America, and the majority are passengers on an Old Age Express living under the influence of the Premature Aging Virus™. The following is a list of some of the key elements in your environment that feed the virus.

### Advertisers

You may not actively listen or watch the advertisements on television however your subconscious is taking it all in. Advertising companies use stereotyping and categorizing when designing their campaigns. This is because it is the most expeditious way to make their pitch in sixty seconds. A stereotype is a generally accepted set of characteristics defining a group. As individuals we also use stereotypes and categories to make sense of the world. We know that people are individuals and do not always conform to the stereotypical however we generally don't have the time or the inclination to differentiate unless it is of direct relevance to our conscious self. The added unfortunate aspect to stereotyping in advertising is that they often exaggerate the group characteristics that best suit their agenda. The use of stereotypes in advertising applies to all forms of traditional and electronic media.

The exciting lifestyle adverts in the majority of instances depict happy super fit people under the age of thirty-five, and on the odd occasion when an older person participates in the advert their character is depicted as slow, doddery and old fashioned. How many prescription drug adverts portray middle-aged and elderly people in a negative light? Our unconscious responds to this stereotype, translating the images for our mind and enhancing our internal representation of what it is to be young and alive versus old and out of date.

One of the most insidious advertisements is for funeral insurance. One minute you are planning a great week-end away and the next you're feeling guilty about spending your money on a vacation instead of buying funeral insurance. It happens In lightning speed.

Over a week let alone a lifetime, your unconscious is continually bombarded with these types of images and subliminal messages which have a direct effect on your state of mind, and your beliefs.

It is hard to fight the tidal wave of stereotypical advertising but your life may depend on it. Awareness gives you the power to fight back.

**Time for you to do some work:**

Over the next 7 days tally the number of advertisements depicting people over the age of thirty-five in a positive and negative light. Awareness is the first step in the fight for your amazing future. You can't change or fix something if you don't know the problem exists in the first place.

**Television programs**

Unfortunately, most television shows follow the same stereotypical script writing and casting as the advertisers. People who are middle aged or older are depicted as uncomfortable with technology, bumbling, slow and retired. They are usually poorly dressed, do not have a career, forgetful, possibly difficult to get along with but are great baby sitters. In fact, middle-aged and older people are disappearing from our television screens. Program directors are pushing the image that the world is for people under the age of thirty with massive character flaws and great bodies.

A few years ago, leading female actors were complaining that there were not enough roles for them and that hitting 50 was not a good career move. Well we live in a fast world as in 2012, Erin Sullivan the star of 'Legally Blonde' live show, was reported as referring to the dirty 30's in the Star News Online:

> Finally, it's back to New York in August to "hit the ground running again," Sullivan said, half-jokingly complaining that she'll be competing against 19, 20, and 21-year-olds" at the age of "dirty 30."

Looks like only children and teenagers will be starring in our movies and television in the coming years. People over the age of 35 will fade from existence. Once again, your unconscious is picking up on these stereotypes of the young and the not so young. It is translating and adding these interpretations to your core beliefs on aging, and it is these beliefs that have a massive influence on your experience of your environment and your state of mind.

**Time for you to do some work:**

List the number of movies and television shows released over the past couple of years that portray middle-aged and older people as positive role models versus bumbling idiots. I would love to see the list. Remember awareness is your first step in fighting for your future.

## Ageism

> Ageism is the newest and fastest mover in the bias top ten, sitting just below racism and sexism.

Ageism is the community and industry bias against people they feel are too old and sometimes too young for a given scenario.

It is a process of stereotyping and discriminating against people because they are old or older than desirable. From a definitional perspective ageism is like racism or sexism in that it treats people differently based on social group stereotypes.

> Our cultural and structural disregard for older populations "is almost the last prejudice we're allowed to have," says Kathryn Lawler, the director of the Atlanta Regional Commission's Area Agency on Aging. Which is deeply ironic: Not only is aging – if one is blessed with a long life and good health – one of the few truly universal experiences, it is something that is becoming more and more pervasive.

Ageism appears in many forms. The following examples illustrate how the behavior of an older person is described in an ageist manner, whereas the same behavior by a younger person is explained without stereotypes:

- When older people forget someone's name, they are viewed as senile. When a younger person fails to recall a name, we usually say he or she just forgot.

- When an older person complains about life or a particular incident, they are called cranky and difficult, while a younger person may be seen as over sensitive or spoiled.
- If an older person has trouble hearing, he is dismissed as "getting old and senile," rather than simply accepting that people of all ages sometimes have difficulty hearing.

---

Older people face ageism on the job and I believe that this is one of the most prevalent areas where middle-aged and older people are unjustly discriminated against because of their chronological age.

BTW: I have often heard people lament that it is impossible to get a job when you turn 50.

---

The general consensus in industry today is that younger workers are more adaptable and comfortable with technology, they are faster, smarter, and take less sick leave. It is also felt that they relate to the consumer better because they are a member of the youthful consumer groups.

Older workers are viewed overall as:

- less productive and disruptive because it is believed that they do not relate to the younger members of staff,
- more expensive as they are too slow to learn new processes and technology
- less adaptable
- take more time off due to illness, resulting in lost productivity and worse still, negatively impacting on the company's medical insurance costs.

Ageism is a major source of energy for the PAV which in turn further infects your unconscious – it is a vicious circle.

It is understandable that you would start to believe you are no longer useful and are more trouble than you are worth. However, the more you think like this and believe it to be true, the more you alienate yourself from your environment, and the more you feel insecure about interacting with the world around you, so the less you do, and off we go again staying put in your seat on the Old Age Express.

> Fear and insecurity are a vicious one two punch that help to keep you on the Old Age Express where your world slowly becomes smaller and darker, eventually closing in on you altogether.... Roselyn Poon

A very clever friend in Australia was having trouble getting work. He had a terrific resume and great references but he couldn't even get an interview. He asked me to read his resume to see if I could work out what the problem was. I reviewed it and suggested he remove his date of birth. The way I saw it, his date of birth was irrelevant information and added nothing to his resume as he had years of verifiable experience. You guessed it, within a week he had a job interview and a new contract. It turned out to be a win-win for everyone.

Ageism in the work force is not an easily won battle, however you as an individual can outsmart ageism with your own PAV cure.

**Time for you to do some work:**

List the number of areas and instances where you feel that you have been personally subjected to ageism or observed it around you.

This is an important list because we are going to use this to help create your personal Premature Aging Cure.

**Groups**

A group is a collection of entities with something in common, in this instance we are talking about people, e.g. members of a Toastmaster group by definition have an interest in public speaking or the Over 50 Club which implies by definition that you need to be over 50 to enjoy this club. This age-based club may work for some people and on the surface, it sounds logical but does it work for you? Are you the stereotypical over 50?

We mentioned earlier during our discussion on ageism that we use stereotypes to help us make sense of the world around us in a timely manner. Groups are a great example of our use of stereotypical assumptions. We consciously and unconsciously make assumptions about groups and hence group members on a regular basis; e.g. what comes to mind when someone you meet says that they belong to a hiking group or a knitting group. Instantly without having any personal experience of the group or the members, you immediately come up with your own interpretation of what the group and its members are probably like. Having made your assumptions, you will respond to the group and its members in accordance with your beliefs about the group's characteristics. Unfortunately, not only do we make assumptions but we react based on these assumptions. This is normal human behavior and there is no real problem in doing this, provided that you are aware that you are generalizing and stereotyping.

This concept cuts both ways, in that people until they get to know you as an individual will make assumptions about you, and will treat you in accordance with their beliefs about the groups you belong to.

The tricky thing is that sometimes we act in accordance with how we are treated. If someone treats us as elderly, our unconscious self-picks up on this, and if this occurs often enough, we will start to believe that we are elderly, and start acting and thinking accordingly.

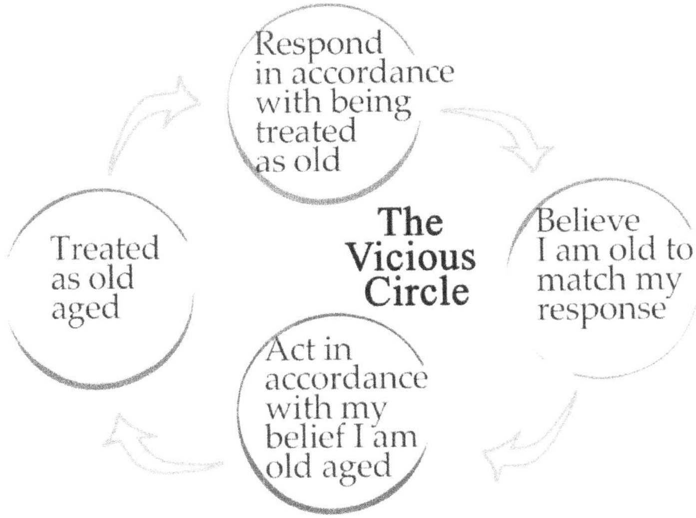


It is a vicious circle – we act, we think, we believe, we act, we think, we believe – the good news is that if we act, think and believe with the intention of being 10 years younger we can use this circle to reclaim our lost years.

We can use the association and stereotyping system in our favor. We just have to bring our actions, thoughts and beliefs to the forefront for a while so our conscious and unconscious selves are working together and reprogramming our mind.

**Time for you to do some work:**

What group's do you belong to or align yourself with, and what are the principal characteristics of the group members?

Do you conform 100% with your description of the other members?

Can you identify people in these groups who do and don't conform to the status quo of the group?

Can you think of instances where you have reacted to someone strictly based on their group affiliation without learning who they are as an individual?

Have you encountered instances where someone has treated you in a manner which you did not appreciate simply based on your affiliations?

## Associations

This is similar to groups in that strangers will make assumptions about you and respond to you based on the people you associate with. The stereotype strikes again.

When we belong to a group or associate with a particular group of people or person for that matter, we have a tendency to align our thoughts and behaviors. It is human nature to want to belong and relate to one another.

> My favorite saying is "like animals herd together, it is not often that you see a Zebra hanging out with a monkey", Zebras hang with Zebras, and so it goes for we humans... Roselyn

**Time for you to do some work:**

Who do you normally associate with?

Have your views and beliefs changed over time to be in alignment with your friends and associates, or are you finding it more difficult to relate to them?

## Language and terminology

The terms senior citizen and seniors have been around for decades and commonly refer to people who are 60+ years of age. The general assumption is that seniors are people who have reached that stage in life referred to as old age. 60+ is that point in time when the government 'old-age' benefit program kicks in.

> BTW: Interestingly, the old-age benefits come from the federal Old-Age, Survivors and Disability Insurance program.

These stereotypical definitions of old-age, senior citizen, senior and retirement have been with us for centuries however our environment has changed considerably and it does not serve us to maintain these outdated roles.

---

*BTW: One of our most toxic outdated beliefs is the retirement age of 65. This was introduced by Prince Otto Von Bismarck and the German government in 1889. They wanted to show their citizens that they were a benevolent government so they introduced the concept of retirement and retirement benefits. In hindsight it was obvious that the Prince had no intention of paying out as they set the retirement age at 65 knowing full well that life expectancy at that point in time was 49 at best.*

---

Recently governments have started moving the retirement age further into the future and at the time of writing this book the official retirement age in the USA and Australia is based on your date of birth. It is still around 66 – 70 years of age.

Our environment and life expectancy have changed considerably over the past one hundred and twenty years, however the majority of us have not updated our thinking.

We are complacent passengers sitting in the Old Age Express with our family and friends happily zooming through the years.

**Financial institutions**

Financial institutions are also complicit in the propagation of the PAV. Surprising isn't it? How do these large commercial entities benefit from aging us prematurely? Revenue of course.

We know that we would do more to avoid pain than to experience pleasure, and that fear is our principal driver. The reality is that life insurance companies and medical insurance companies also know this and it forms the basis for their most effective income earning strategies.

---

BTW: The earlier insurance companies scare us into believing we are moving into old age, the earlier they start earning money from our premiums and contributions.

---

These companies have a vested interest in convincing us that we are rapidly growing old, and that with old age comes a host of expensive illnesses and life or death events that we need to insure against.

They paint a fearful picture of what it is to be old and the earlier they can convince us of this, the more profitable their bottom line becomes. The reality is that we are subjected to these types of advertisements and sales tactics on a daily basis. Our unconscious quietly takes these negative messages on board and eventually our beliefs about ourselves and our mortality are negatively impacted.

> Once our beliefs change, our experience of the world around us changes and so follows our future ...Roselyn

**Friends and family**

We get on with our day to day living until one day a comment or an event triggers the PAV into action. A friend might remark how they are starting to feel the aches and pains of old age, or the headline on a magazine cover screams "What the celebs are doing to stop Father Time", or even more disturbing is the news that a friend, relative, or colleague has just died.

I am not saying that you should avoid your family and friends. I am just asking that you become aware of the impact their age-related comments and feelings have on your state of mind.

> BTW: Personally, I avoid the New Year's Eve list of famous people who have died over the past year – it fills me with sadness at the loss to the world and a feeling that my life's journey thus far is a little more faded.

**Technology**

---

BTW: This is a good one because technology is moving so fast that even youngsters in their 30's are starting to feel old and outdated.

---

The rate of change of technology is enough to make anyone feel outdated and over the hill. If you let it.

I believe that the biggest problem is the terminology. Technology has always been shrouded in mystery with its own secret language. I come from the world of technology, so I know first-hand that mystery suits the members of this technology club. It allows them to maintain their feeling of superiority over us mere mortals and hold us to ransom.

Normally you wouldn't feel old or inferior if you didn't understand what someone was saying when they were speaking in a foreign language. You accept the fact that it is a language you are not familiar with and ask for help in translation. No problem.

Why is it then so hard to ask for help when dealing with 'techno babble'? Why do we instantly feel outdated aka old, if we don't understand? I believe it is because we believe they are speaking in our native tongue, and what they are saying is so simple that a child can grasp it in seconds, so we must be getting too old to keep up. WRONG! They being the media, other people and other sources of information are speaking 'techno babble'. It may as well be Martian and if it was, you would not berate yourself for not understanding.

Techno Babble is a subset of our native tongue. It is comprised of words, phrases, abbreviations otherwise referred to as acronyms, syntax, and expressions that have been created by the IT industry. Truthfully, they need to create these new words and phrases to describe new processes and devices however it can be interpreted.

I use Google all of the time to help me better understand what is going on in the world. It is particularly helpful with translating acronyms and unfamiliar terminology.

---

BTW: The problem is not our level of intelligence or our age. The problem is the language.

---

Please ask for help in understanding technology and bear in mind you don't have to know how or why things work, you just need to know how to use them. Start small and ask Google. The first few hours or days will be the hardest but you are clawing back your life so get on with it.

Every human on this Earth at some point had to start learning how to use the latest technology. The only difference between you and them is the point in your timeline when it became a priority to ask and learn.

---

BTW: All joking aside, there is a real problem with fearing the expansion of technology in our world. Technology is not going away and very soon nearly everything we do will be underpinned or delivered by some kind of technology.

If you don't overcome your fear of the unknown for fear of looking stupid you will progressively become isolated from the rest of the world. For most of us, there is no upside to isolation. The more isolated you become the more fearful you become causing further isolation and so it goes.

---

## Activating the Premature Aging Virus

During your first 40 – 50 stations the PAV has been fairly dormant. Quietly fed by your surroundings and the people you associate with. It could lay dormant for your entire life but I doubt it. Sooner or later an emotional trigger will set it off and you will start to feel older each day.

*BTW: The PAV is similar to a number of human biological viruses that lay dormant until a trigger sets it off, e.g. varicella-zoster virus which cause shingles and chickenpox*

Common PAV triggers are:

- The first time someone refers to you as a senior citizen, or the older generation.
- The first time someone says that you are too old to apply for their job vacancy.
- The first time someone says, "You won't understand because you are too old".
- The first time you wished that you could have your time over again.
- When someone asks if you have considered your retirement options.
- When someone wants to know when you are moving into a retirement village.
- When you decide not to pursue a course of study or a project because you simply feel that there is not enough time to see it through.
- Retirement.
- Retrenchment.
- Bankruptcy, economic downturn.
- Kids leaving home.
- Your 50th, 60th birthday.
- Key wedding anniversary.
- Becoming a grandparent.
- The death of your life partner, someone close, or colleague.
- Just feeling tired and run down.

The list goes on forever. Some of the triggers just wake it up and others set it off with a vengeance, e.g. the death of someone close to you will more than likely have you estimating how many years you have to go, which has a rapid flow on effect to other considerations and decisions based on the number you come up with.

Other triggers like the graduation of your youngest child will give you pause to reflect, albeit just for a split second on where you are in your life and what is left.

**Time for you to do some work:**

List at least 10 events that you believe could set the PAV off causing you to consider your age, your life, your regrets, your accomplishments.

Think about your future and write a note to yourself describing what you see ahead and how you feel about it.

Our knowledge largely consists of what we've learned over time-what we've read, heard, and seen. A lot of the input that makes up our library of knowledge is actually just other people's opinions. Imagine that. Perhaps 50 percent of the dialog chugging along in your mind is made up of other people's opinions! Opinions are a powerful influence when they find a fertile mind. ..... Ray Dodd Author of The Power of Belief

# Chapter 3

## The Pain of Old Age

> You can't help getting older, but you don't have to get old.... George Burns

The great thing about the PAV is that the cure is based on the same elements that created it in the first place:

- your state of mind
- your environment
- your beliefs about aging
- your beliefs about where you are in your time line
- your picture of your future

So far, we have seen how a great deal of your life runs on autopilot which is necessary if you are to get through the day; however, some aspects of your life need your consideration and control. Generally, the people in your environment think and act similarly, hence if the status quo thinking with regards to aging is that we all age at the same rate, then the issue of aging is considered a non-issue and accepted as normal. You believe that old age and death are just facts of life so your subconscious doesn't waste time thinking about it.

I agree getting old eventually leads to death, and we all die eventually, but I believe we can delay the miserable old age phase for years. Wouldn't you like to be as young as possible until the very last minute? The good news is that as long as you are breathing you have a chance.

> Death is a certainty, but you don't have to spend a third of your life going through old age to get there... Roselyn

**Extend your youthful life and kick old age to the curb**

The two most important things I learned from Tony Robbins are:

- We will do more to escape PAIN than to receive PLEASURE.
- We need a big enough WHY to change.

My life changing pain was brought about when I looked into my future and saw a nightmare:

- I saw retirement as the start of a slow death and I was a breath away
- I did not have enough money to live on when I retired
- No more opportunities to achieve things that I wanted to do
- Loss of my independence
- Haunted by feelings that I had let myself down
- Nothing I could do except simply survive.
- The color was dark and the outlook was bleak

I could feel the pain and heartbreak. I could feel the despair and sadness. The feeling of just killing time until the end was devastating. I could see the endless grey days ahead of me. I could feel the emptiness. It was a horror movie running in my mind and it gave me my big enough WHY. I had to save myself from a miserable, lonely depressing slow death.

My pain was so severe and real that I experienced an epiphany and took action immediately. Not after lunch, not tomorrow, not when I had attended to all those little things on my to-do list but immediately. Within seconds I was a changed person and took control of my time line and future. I realized that I could be any age I wanted to be and that no one had the right to tell me otherwise.

It has not all been clear sailing since the epiphany. Sometimes the going gets a bit tough, but all I need to do is think about the nightmarish alternative and I am back in the driver's seat living my life.

I love my life. I love the fact that I have clawed back 20 years of my life at a critical time and I have many years to go. It didn't cost me anything other than understanding that time is a construct and it is malleable. I learned to bend time to suit me and completely changed my beliefs regarding aging and where I am in my time line.

Roselyn and girlfriends at her fashion company party, 2018. Roselyn second from the right.

The magic is to keep focused on living younger for longer no matter what, and to this end you need to create a big enough WHY. The alternative to reframing your beliefs about time and aging has to be less painful than staying on the Old Age Express and living over a third of your life in the old age category.

Your WHY is where it all starts so let's begin with the painful question of what old age means to you.

## What is age?

According to the latest trends there are 4 ways of gauging your age:

- Chronological – the number of years you have lived
- Biological – how old you seem based on standard biomarkers
- Social – this is age stratification aka the hierarchical ranking of people into **age** groups within a society, e.g. old age, middle age, teen agers, etc.
- Psychological – this represents how old you actually feel or act.

**Chronological age** is simply the number of years you have been alive. It is a system of measurement and of no importance to who you are. Remember, chronological age is just a page number in your book of life. It has no bearing on the content of your book. It has no effect on the plot or the characters. It just provides you with a point of reference for particular events, e.g. the butler found the body in the library on page 147. Similarly, after childhood your age should have no more bearing on the events in your life other than providing you with a date stamp for your life's events, e.g. on page 27 Roselyn divorced Peter, on page 42 Roselyn started competitive Porsche racing.

**Biological or physiological age** refers to the physical changes that accompany the aging process. Today you can be tested to determine your body's biological age; how much wear and tear there is on your heart, liver and kidneys, etc.

It is not uncommon to have a difference between your biological and chronologic ages. Biological aging is impacted by heredity and your lifestyle, whereas chronological age is just a sequential numbering system.

**Social age** promotes ageism which feeds the Premature Aging Virus. It refers to the changes in a person's roles and relationships as the person ages in accordance with their environment. It is stratification which allows the use of stereotyping, e.g. middle age and old age. If living younger for longer is your focus you must ignore the age classifications, and in particular not buy into the social age classification titled 'old age'.

**Psychological age** is the age you believe yourself to be. This is the age we are focused on because this is where the magic is. Pushing your psychological age to the forefront and updating your beliefs about aging is the principal source of the cure for the Premature Aging Virus PAV.

> BTW: It is common for your mind to make a quantum leap when it comes to aging. One minute you are sitting in a traffic jam with nowhere to go and you start to think. "I am 45 years old, nearly the big 5 0, heading for retirement and the old people's home. Only a few years left." ... Roselyn Poon

**Your psychology is all powerful**

Have you ever imagined yourself in the future, or through circumstances made a quantum leap into the older you?
e.g.

- You are minding your own business when suddenly you start to think about the number of years you have left in your life.
- Maybe you just experienced a mild heart attack and now all you can think about for the next few weeks is your pending death.
- Maybe you think about being middle aged and your mind goes into free fall to old age.

It is true what they say about your mind not knowing the difference between reality and truth. Regularly jumping to thinking about retirement and old age before your time will eventually cause your mind to believe that you are already retired and old, which in turn has an enormous bearing on how you see the world and your experience of it. The point of view of someone who believes they are 70 is quite different to someone who believes they are 50.

Think of how much you have achieved and learned (both good and bad) during the last few years, and then think about how much you have still got to go if you claw back a few extra years now. It should take your breath away.

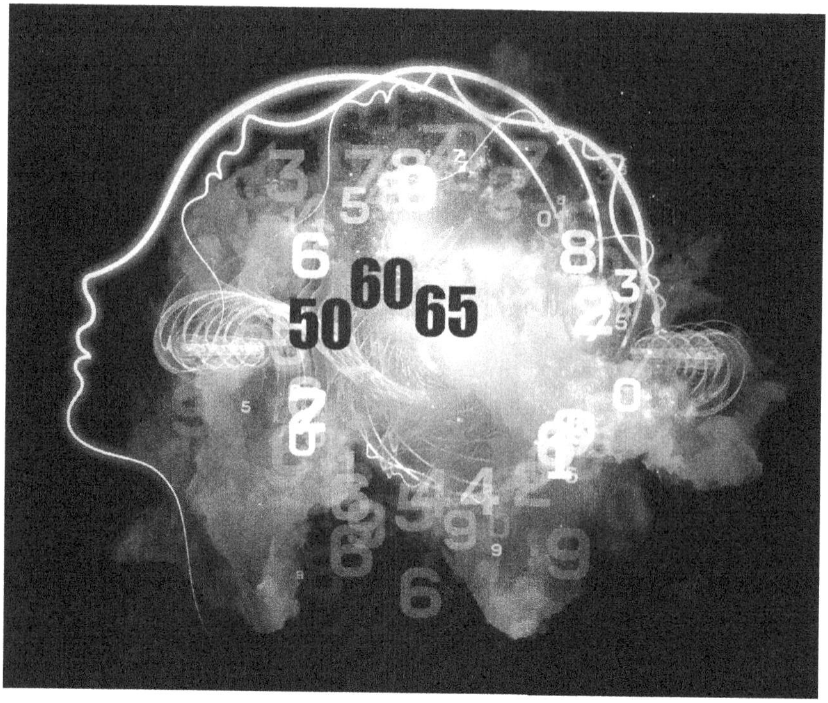


If it took you 30 years to advance five spots on the Monopoly Board of Life starting at ground zero, just think how much faster you will be able to advance five spots given your accumulated experience, wisdom, hindsight, assets and younger state of mind. With your accumulated wealth of knowledge and experience you can even change tracks completely with the confidence that you are not starting from scratch.

I originally recalibrated my inner clock from 45 to 32. This instantly gave me an extra 13 valuable youthful years to change my future. It felt incredible to feel 32 and have the hind-site and knowledge of someone with 13 more years of experience.

How would you feel if you took 10 years off your age this minute? Try it. Close your eyes and say to yourself that when you open your eyes you will be 10 years younger. Keeping that age how do you see your current circumstances? Personally, I released a massive amount of stress about retirement and felt relief that I now had time to change my future.

Most people think that growing old is inevitable, which it is, however most of us speed up the process and provide very little resistance. The older we get the more we ponder and stress about time and aging. The more we worry about aging the older we get.

You can slow down your aging through controlling your state of mind and beliefs about your aging. Feed your younger enthusiastic energized psychological age and live younger longer.

---

Control your destiny through your state of mind... Roselyn Poon

---

Remember, your mind does not know the difference between what is real and imagined. This is why the PAV creates such havoc with your aging process, but you are going to turn the tables on the PAV and use this mind over matter theory to your advantage.

If you allow your mind to continually refer to yourself as senior, old, getting old, too old to do this or that, too late to start something, you are training your mind to believe this is your real-life situation.

Ultimately your mind believes that you are too old and this state of mind will affect your decisions and how you respond to the world. You will make decisions based on being much older than you really are.

---

You have psychologically prematurely aged yourself -- aka -- you have an active PAV.

---

The good news is that you can change your psychological age for free. It takes personal effort and a big enough why to make the changes. The wonder is that the magic is in your hands.

## *Can I See Me*

If I could see me
the way you see me,
What would I be?
Why does my mirror lie to me?
Flaws, only flaws, that's all I see.
Pain and weakness.
Fear in me.
Inadequate–imperfect.
Everything I am not.

If I could step outside of me,
if I could only see me, the way you see me,
what would I be?
A knight, a prince, royalty?
Strong and bold.
Fearless and brave.
A gift from heaven
here to save.

If I could see me
the way you see me,
what would I be?
Free.

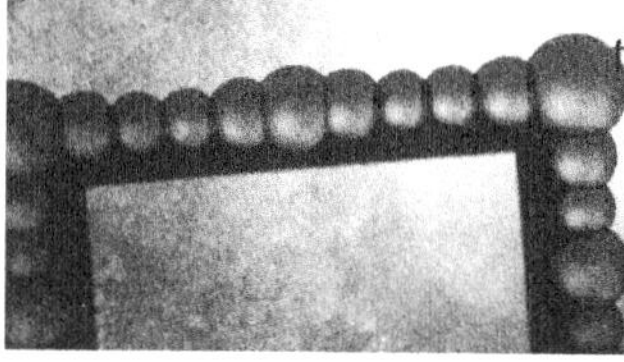

*Jeff Manning*

**from The Dream Builder by Jeff Manning**

## When Does Old Age Start?

I believe most people think old age starts when they retire, however it depends on the psychological perspective you have about aging. Some people think they're in old age when they're 40 or 50. I even know some 30-year-olds who believe they have missed the boat.

It is widely accepted that once we are in our 60's we are in the old age strata, and the next stop is death sometime in our 80's or when our parents passed away, discounting illness and accidents. The truth is it depends on whether you're male or female, your cultural environment, your DNA, your overall health, lifestyle, level of stress and most importantly, your state of mind.

The generalization that most people pass away by the time they're in their 80s is a misnomer. We are conditioned to think this applies to us, but it only applies if you believe it. I for one certainly do not believe my adventures will end in my 80's. I'm going to be around until I'm 120 years of age. That's me. That's my story and I'm sticking to it.

I believe that most of us accept our ultimate termination; however, we want to be as young and functioning as possible until that time. This is a terrific aspiration however you need to turn it into a reality, and that takes work and a change in your mind set starting today.

> You have a choice. You can run your own race or stay with the other passengers on the Old Age Express.... Roselyn

## What Does Old Age Have to Offer?

> Old age is no place for sissies.... Bette Davis Actor

Beware, old age sneaks up on you, one minute at a time. It is a process over time, during which you keep making seemingly minor insignificant adjustments to your lifestyle, until one day the infamous straw that broke the camel's back hits you and you realize that you have reached old age.

Don't let old age ambush you. Being forewarned is forearmed.... Roselyn

The following is a brief look at some of the issues that will arise leading up to and during old age. Most can occur at any time however they are more prevalent and intense during classic old age. I am not saying that the following issues can be totally avoided. However, with some work on your state of mind and state of being, you can delay the onset of old age, and maybe even completely avoid some of the issues experienced by the elderly.

**Everyday life issues**

Think about the last time you woke up feeling tired, blurry vision and muscle sore. Not a great start to the day, however after a couple of vitamin B capsules you know you will be back to normal pretty quickly. Now imagine waking up every day feeling that way, with the added knowledge that there is no quick fix, and wondering if you will speak to anyone today.

Remember how difficult simple things were when you had your arm, leg or some other body part in a plaster cast or heavily bandaged. I bet that was the longest six weeks of your life. Now think about having this kind of challenge every day for the rest of your life. If you really want a wake-up call add this difficulty and frustration to the feelings in the previous paragraph. It is enough to make you want to stay in bed forever, and sadly a lot of old aged people do exactly that.

Most elderly people find even the simplest tasks, such as dressing, reading, getting to the doctor, answering the phone, showering, and pushing a grocery cart challenging, on an ongoing basis. They do this believing that things are only going to get worse.

Paying bills and keeping up with the ever-changing government forms that need to be completed and filed each year is hard enough for you now, so imagine what it will be like ten or fifteen years from now.

Everyday tasks that you currently have no problem with, and in fact don't even think about, represent challenges, barriers and limitations for our elderly and maybe even the future you.

---

Personal story: My mother is 87 and sadly she lives in Australia and I live in the USA. Recently her little car broke down so the family took the opportunity to take away her driver's license. They gave her a cell phone and explained that when she wanted to go out all she needed to do is call Uber and the driver will take her anywhere she wants to go. They also said she did not have to pay because the fare would be charged to the family account.

Sounds easy doesn't it? I called her and asked how it was going and she cried. She couldn't go to the Medicare office because she didn't know how to use the cell phone. The family had given her an explanation on how to use it, and left.

I called a niece and asked her to drop around and go through it with her a few times and in fact take a ride with her. When I called mum to see how it went, she said that my niece was not able to teach her because the mobile was not charged.

---

It turns out no one had explained to mum that unlike her house phone, this mobile phone needed to be plugged into the socket and charged.

I know it is hard for you to see yourself in this situation when you are in your 80's, however the world is changing at an incredible pace so who knows what challenges are ahead. Until my mother can learn how to call Uber, her world will end at her front door. Last week she was a happy independent little lady driving her car around her neighborhood staying in touch with the outside world, and in less than a week she has become house bound and dependent on others through no fault of her own. Each day her world becomes slightly smaller.

Let's talk about dignity and self-respect. Wouldn't your self-esteem take a serious hit if people patronized you, excluded you from decision-making about your own life, and basically treated you as an object or an issue to be resolved? Add to this an overall feeling of vulnerability because your life is no longer your own. Is this the future you want? Now is the time to do something about the future you. Reset your inner clock and start working at being more youthful and in control of your life.

How do you maintain your independence when everything around you is constantly changing and becoming alien to you? By the time you are in the old age category the roads may well be packed with driverless vehicles. Driving rules would have probably changed to meet the new driverless cars and unless your car is electric it may not even be allowed on the roads. Just last week I heard on the news that New Zealand is looking into applying a tax on cars that use fossil fuel. Think about it.

These are just some of the issues elderly people face every day until they die. I want you to confront old age and feel it. I want you to take control of your aging now and work at keeping it at bay for as long as possible or at least the last few years. The most important question to ask yourself is do you want to stay on the Old Age Express or jump off and take control of your future?

**Possible health issues**

Regardless of the body you have now it will be very different in 10 – 20 years' time. Changes will occur in spite of medical advancements because there are many non-biological issues that affect how we age, not the least of which are environmental and genetic.

At the time of writing this book, 2019, the most widespread conditions affecting those 65 and older include arthritis, heart disease, stroke, cancer, pneumonia, stress and the flu. Accidents, especially falls that result in hip fractures, are also unfortunately common in the elderly.

Over the coming years you may expect to be confronted with one or more of the following health issues:

- Heart conditions (hypertension, high blood pressure and coronary artery disease)
- Dementia, including Alzheimer's disease
- Depression
- Incontinence (urinary and bowel)
- Arthritis & Osteoporosis
- Frequent falls, which can lead to fractures and feelings of insecurity
- Eye problems (cataracts, glaucoma, Macular Degeneration)
- A weakened immune system, which can make fighting off viruses, bacteria and diseases difficult.

This is just a sample and by no means inclusive. You may be thinking that your current lifestyle and level of fitness puts you above these and that is great if that is the case. This puts you ahead of the pack and I commend you. Your state of mind is already addressing these issues, but I urge you to read on as there may be some new issues around the corner.

BTW: One in eight baby boomers will get the Alzheimer disease after they turn 65. At age 85 that risk increases to nearly one in two. And if they don't have it, chances are they will likely be caring for someone who does. For many baby boomers, Alzheimer's was a disease they saw in their parents or grandparents. Not anymore. Alzheimer's disease is now their disease, their crisis, their epidemic.

Alzheimer's disease is not just a little memory loss. It eventually kills you, but not before it takes everything away — slowly, gradually, painstakingly, inevitably. This devastating, deteriorating and debilitating disease is the ultimate thief — thief of memories, thief of independence, thief of control, thief of time and ultimately thief of life.

Alzheimer's robs people of all bodily functions and eventually their humanity. Day by day, Alzheimer's strips away individuality, autonomy and independence. It means the loss of anything and everything you have ever known.... Alzheimer's Association 2011, www.alz.org

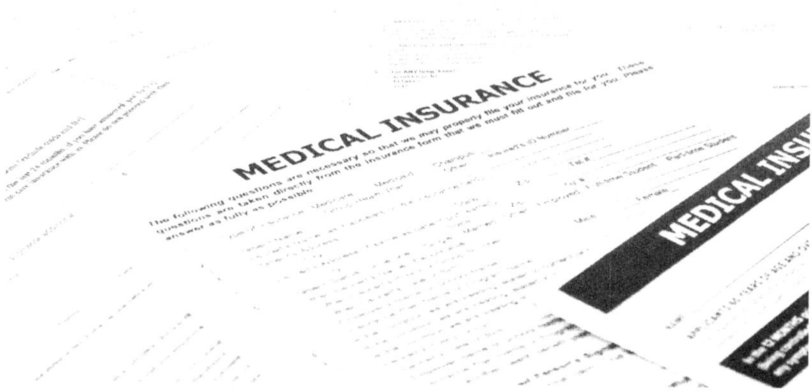


**Medicare and government forms**

Now that we are talking about medical issues, we must add medical insurance into the equation. Think about how difficult it is to navigate your way through all the red tape today when you are reasonably up to date and fighting fit. What will it be like in 10 years-time when your need is greatest and you are less equipped to handle the process and the myriad of forms and procedures?

Working on your more youthful state of mind now, will help you to stave off old age to the last minute, and when it does arrive, you will be much stronger mentally, and in better condition to fight back.

Old age is a wonderful time of life. At least, that's what everyone tells you. But let me tell you: it is not true. What's true is that your hips, knees and ankles gradually give up on you - everything is quite dreadful, really. And it was a terrible thing to have told us because we believed it... Debbie Reynolds Actor

---

**Possible financial issues**

The most unfortunate aspect to retiring and depending on the government or my investment funds is that we can never truly know what is coming around the corner. Case in point is the 2007 Global Financial Crisis. I tip my hat to you if you are one of the fortunate ones who managed to get through the 2007 Global Financial Crisis unscathed. Sadly, a large number of 401(K) and personal contribution pension/superannuation plans took a big hit. The retirees living on the monthly payments took the brunt, and of course they are the ones least able to recover because they are considered elderly or senior citizens meaning un-employable.

I am sure you have heard a lot of horror stories about people losing their homes because they suddenly found themselves underwater with their mortgage. Housing values plummeted, employment dropped, returns on investments dropped, renters defaulted, etc. It takes a long time to recover from these types of financial crisis especially if you have already mentally retired. I have incredible respect for the elderly who have fought back and found jobs doing tasks they never would have imagined, e.g. cleaning, collecting supermarket trolleys, serving at fast food chains.

Revisit your nest egg. If you don't have one, I suggest you start today. Working on inserting an extra 10 years into your timeline right now will help you to build that nest egg. Old age is hard enough without adding financial burden to the mix. Think about the rise in living costs that will occur during your old age.

---

BTW: I was recently in a supermarket when I noticed the checkout girl asking the elderly man in front of me to decide on a loaf of bread or a carton of milk. He didn't have enough money for both. I quietly interrupted her and paid for his groceries. He was very thankful but I could see the embarrassment in his eyes. He wasn't homeless or unkempt he was simply caught short by the daily increase in the cost of living... Roselyn

---

Government support for the elderly is also looking tenuous as the retiree population expands faster than ever expected.

BTW: When the retirement security benefit was introduced in 1935, the average life expectancy was just around 62, lower than the retirement age, which, even then, was still 65. The proportion of adults collecting social security was significantly lower when the benefit was introduced, and they would live, on average, for fewer years after stopping work. Now, that's not the case, and the safety net is stretched to snapping. Among the middle age and younger populations, anxiety about caregiving responsibilities is growing." ........ Kathryn Lawler, director of the Atlanta Regional Commission's Area Agency on Aging.

Living younger for longer may help you to stay in the work force longer so that you can rebuild or add to your war chest. It is never too late to start preparing for old age, and the longer you can defer that time the better off you are.

I have covered just a few of the areas that have the potential to cause you grief when you are elderly. I am sure there are many more. The point is to bring it to your attention. Your body and intellect will change over time along with your environment so start preparing now.

## When Does Society Classify You as Old Aged or Elderly?

We need to adjust our overall attitude toward growing old. As a culture, we tend to treat aging as a separate phase, not an extension of the same life. "You see people in retirement communities and they're infantilized, spoken to as if they were infants even though they've lived these rich lives and had remarkable experiences," ...... Paul Irving, the chair of the Center for the Future of Aging at the Milken Institute.

I focus on living younger; however, it was my quick trip into what old age had to offer me that inspired and continually motivates me to keep living younger.

I think most people believe they have transitioned into the old age category when they have retired or when their life partner retires.

BTW: *Retirement* is *defined* as seclusion or privacy, or withdrawal from work due to age. An example of *retirement* is going into a back bedroom and taking a nap. ..... YourDictionary.com

Traditionally, retirement is seen as either a time when you can relax and take up some of the things you have always wanted to do or a period of confusion and loneliness. Retirement is a whole book on its own, however today I just want to look at it from the perspective of the affect it has on feeding the PAV.

The more important question to ask is when did you or when will you see yourself as a member of the old age strata?

Old age and the definition of old age are affected by all sorts of factors. Apart from retirement the next best old age trigger is when the government tells you that you are now in the old age category of society. You get a little card in the mail that says, "You're now a senior citizen and we thank you for all your years of endeavor. We're going to give you a 10% discount on your railway pass and utility bills as well as a small regular social security check to help you to get by." These are just some of the things that help to make us believe that we're too old to make a difference to our life and future.

Regardless of what triggers an old age state of mind, it is a very personal thing. Some people think they're in old age when they're 40 or 50. I have met 30-year-olds who believe they are too old to still be relevant, and 80-year-olds who believe they are just getting started.

BTW: I refuse to have anything to do with senior discount tickets at the movie theatre. I would much rather pay $16 or whatever it happens to be, than actually go up and say, I'm a senior citizen. No! In my mind, I'm not a senior citizen. That's one of the prices I have to pay for being younger than my age.

I believe old age is that time when you know that you have done it all, and you are ready to sit on the beach with a good book and watch the world go by.

*BTW: I plan to start being a life spectator on my 110th birthday... Roselyn*

Roselyn's mother Alice Poon age 87

## Getting in Touch with Your Old Age

If you are finding it difficult to get a feeling for what it is going to be like to be old aged, I suggest talking to older relatives, neighbors or paying a visit to your local elderly/senior citizen's care facility. You don't need to interrogate them to get a feeling for what their life is like. Just strike up a conversation explaining that you are interested in some of the issues you may have when you are their age. Let them say what they want to say and be sensitive to their state of mind and emotions.

---

Personal story: During the final editing phase of this book I was staying with my mother for a few weeks over Christmas. She had recently lost her license and independence. She was told by everyone that she was too old to drive and she was even taken to her doctor who ratified the family consensus.

Mother believed they were right and has since taken on the state of mind of a little elderly lady. I am shocked at the decline in her overall state of mind. She shuffles around bent over, and is obviously starting to get a little confused as she asks for confirmation about family members and what is going on around her. She is still very active around her home and delights in going to the supermarket where she still has some control over what she sees and buys however this is a couple of hours a week.

The saddest thing of all is when she sits in her armchair and teases me about leaving her. She says that she sits alone in her chair every-day now, but she doesn't bare a grudge with the family because she now believes she is too old to drive and they were looking after her when they took her license away.

---

During my research I came across a great review from two people who participated in a day long exercise on what it is like to be old aged. The exercise was designed to help careers better understand the issues faced by the elderly under their care.

BTW: As part of the Older Adult Sensitivity Training Program, we wore funny-looking glasses that simulated conditions like glaucoma and cataracts and donned bulky gloves that imitated arthritic hands. I immediately realized that what I had previously considered easy tasks, like buttoning a shirt, opening a medication bottle or handling small pills, suddenly required my full concentration and took twice as long to complete. That is, if I could complete them at all.

I knew getting old was difficult, but before this simulation, I didn't fully grasp the complexities of dealing with declining physical and mental capabilities. I can't imagine the fear that must coincide with knowing there's nothing you can do to turn back time.

At the end of the course, I could take off my vision-impairing glasses and dexterity-impeding gloves and get on with my life at a "normal" pace, but my aging parents have to cope with those hurdles every day for the rest of their lives.

I can tell you this much: Put yourself in an elderly person's shoes, even for just five minutes, and you will gain a better understanding of what it's like to grow older and greater appreciation for what seniors deal with. It was an eye-opening experience.... Marlo Sollitto, AgingCare.com contributor

Now is the time to be brave and look into your future as it stands today. All things being equal as people often say.

**Time for you to do some work:**

Feel what it is like to be old aged. Visualization alone is not going to do it. You need to FEEL IT to get the full affect, and you need the full affect to help build your big enough reason why you need to change your state of mind regarding aging.

Try some of the things Marlo Sollitto did:

- smear a small amount of Vaseline or cooking oil over the lenses of your glasses to emulate failing eye sight

- try wearing rubber gloves all day and feel how hard it is to use your keyboard or your cell

- stuff your ears with cotton wool and try participating in conversations

- turn the volume down to barely audible

- try restricting your mobility by tying your knees together loosely and walking around home, even after 10 minutes your frustration level will be through the roof

These are just a few physical things you can do to get some of the feeling going. Add to this, feelings of alienation and isolation, loss of self-esteem, and independence.

How would you feel if some of your family and friends you socialize with and have some connection with are no longer around?

How would you feel if others started making decisions for you?

What would it be like if your neighborhood changed, as people move on and new people take their place?

You need to take some time to dig deep. You are trying to build a safe and exciting future for yourself, but you need to get firmly in touch with what could happen if you don't act now.

Give yourself a break, no one else is going to... Roselyn

## Racing Toward Old Age

I believe the speed of aging is faster today than ever. People keep telling us 50 is the new 30. Well that might be well and good when it comes to advertising, but, in fact, what I've discovered is as each generation comes along, technology is increasing in speed and can single handedly age you in a nanosecond, if you let it.

Today's 40-year-olds, already feel that they're on the way out because they're no longer up-to-date with the 20-year-olds. Whereas a couple of years ago, these 40-year-olds were 30, and they thought they were the rulers of the universe. Now, suddenly they're 40, and they're starting to feel that they're over the hill. This is a really interesting sociological issue that's happening now.

Honestly, they need to be just as aware, as you and I that aging happens to everyone. Getting old, growing old and thinking old are states of being that we have some control over. In fact, we have a lot of control over it.

Stop racing around like headless chickens. We are so caught up with what we have to do, where we have to be next and trying to keep up with the rest of the crowd that we don't even have time to stop and think, "Are we are rushing towards the goal we really want?"

## Where Are You Right Now?

The first thing you need to do before you start on a journey of your choosing is to know where you are to begin with. The great thing about taking the time to work out where your starting point is before going too far is that you increase your chances of successfully getting to your destination before time runs out.

---

Personal story: I learned the importance of knowing where you are before mapping out a route from car rallying. I used to be a racing driver and one of my favorite events was the five-day Dutton's Rally. It was usually through rural Victoria and South Australia, so there were no road signs. There was a driver and a navigator in each car, and throughout the day we would race from one check point to another. At the start line of each check point my navigator would be handed our instruction sheet for this section. Using the sheet, she would have to solve a series of cryptic clues to work out where the next check point was, and the route we had to take. My job was to get us there on time and skillfully execute the crazy driving tests upon arrival.

On the first day at the first check point I screamed off the start line as soon as my navigator received our instructions. Wouldn't you know the start line was on a road that went immediately into a 4 way round about. I spent the first five minutes driving in circles until my navigator could work out which road we had to take to get started. Needless to say, there was much laughter from the spectators and screaming from my navigator. She demanded that I STOP and give her time to work out where we were, but as any race driver will tell you we are deaf as soon as the engine starts □

When we finally turned onto the right road out of town, she explained in no uncertain terms that we had no chance of getting to the destination check point if we didn't know where we were starting from. She made her point and for the remaining checkpoints I sat quietly squeezing the driving wheel with my pent-up adrenalin until she yelled GO!

I am pleased to say that thanks to my clever navigator we aced every route and came in 20th overall. Not bad for an all-girl team going up against over 200 seasoned rally teams... Roselyn

---

Roselyn competing in Australian Porsche Cup

Let's start by getting a realistic perspective on where you are on your life journey. This can be a little disturbing, but it has to be done if you want to increase your chances of getting some of those valuable years back.

**Time for you to do some work:**

Stop reading for a while and map out your Old Age Express train journey thus far. Stop when you get to today. You can make it as detailed as you want. Believe me it isn't as easy to recollect the stations as you might think. You will need this for an exercise in a later chapter.

When you have finished writing up your Old Age Express train line it is a good idea to review it. Take some time to ponder over your journey thus far and maybe you will start to see how you arrived at your current station. Think about the people and places that have had an effect on you and your decisions. Think about some of the alternatives you might have taken if things were different.

Just a little more pain before we get to the pleasure.

Earlier you looked at your Life Train Line from station zero to now. If you bypassed that exercise, I strongly recommend you do it before the next exercise. It is too hard to work out what is coming next, if you don't know where you are now and how you got there.

Now you are going to imagine your future if you do nothing about reframing your beliefs on aging and take back 10 – 20 years.

To get you started I have mapped out what I imagined to be my future time line from Station 40 to the end of the line, prior to jumping off the Old Age Express at station 45.

**My Train Line – Departed Warracknabeal Hospital, April 1, 1953 at 6:15am**

- Station 40 – purchased Porsche race car, IT company still going strong
- Stations 41 – 43 Racing-driver in Porsche Cup Race Series, IT company took a hit from global economic recession.
- Station 45 - realization that I was in for big trouble with retirement just around the corner. Major melt down. Sell Porsche race car and stop racing. Rocky terrain ahead.
- Station 46 – 49 – Panic stations.
- Station 50 – Wind up Computer Link and look for work as a free-lance consultant. Change life style drastically and cut back on travel. Very sad that I am now going through a slow death. Frustration that I picked up the ball too late to do anything with it. The big 5 0 – feeling like it is all downhill from here.
- Station 51 – Work on clearing debts and saving money for retirement. Stressful time for the next 15 years as I head towards retirement and the thought of living on a limited pension. Not able to help family.
- Station 65 – Retirement. Living on a limited pension. Loss of independence. I still have my black Porsche 911 but can't afford to keep it in tip top condition so do not drive it very much. Living in a lower income area than I

was used to. Possibly renting or maybe sharing for the first time in my life. Single. Much quieter life-style. Maybe go back to painting in acrylics.

- Station 70 – Isolated. Parents have passed. Friends have moved on with their lives. Very little interaction with outside.
- Station 80 – Quietly clock out.

**Time for you to do some work:**

Map out your projected time line with the upcoming stations under the assumption that you have no control over your aging.

Be realistic and if possible, include how you are feeling. The important station is retirement, and what happens after that.

To do this effectively you need to understand that your world is constantly changing and over the coming years your finances, health, neighborhood, friends and opportunities will change.

Specifically look at the station five years from now, and then 10 years from now. These are not too far into your future so you should be able to visualize them clearly. At each station consider the following:

- where are you, are you still in the same dwelling and neighborhood?

- what does your environment look like – home, street, job, kids, grandkids, spouse?

- what does your world sound like – noisy, quiet, frantic, relaxing?

- are you following society's time line and associated roles?

- are you following someone else's life course?

- have you made any major changes in your world?

- what is your state of mind – happy, contented, lonely, given up?

- are you traveling alone?

- where are you traveling to?

- do you have regrets? If so, list them.

If the last exercise isn't enough to get you thinking about your future and reconsidering your attitude towards aging and old age, try the next one for size.

**Time for you to do some work:**

How would you feel if you lost your independence?

Do you have people who are dependent on you?

List the 3 worst things that could happen in your life.

If any or all of these events occurred, how would they affect your family, friends, business, community and most of all you?

Is it worthwhile to you and those you hold dear to reduce the likelihood of these events occurring?

Creating a big enough why to reprogram your state of mind on aging often involves considering people close to us as well as ourselves.

What we have been doing up until now is getting a grip on where your Old Age Express is headed, and creating your big enough why to claw back time and take control of your future time line.

Your projections are not set in concrete however you now have a better idea of the general picture of what is coming up. The next chapter is the pleasure side of the coin, looking at your amazing alternative to staying on the Old Age Express.

The Old Age Express
What's your next station?

# Chapter 4

## Your Amazing Alternative to Old Age

Old age isn't a battle; old age is a massacre ...Philip Roth Author

Have you ever woken up from a nights' sleep, and felt tired and exhausted just thinking about the day ahead? Your mind has given you an instant experience of the future, leaving you exhausted before you have time to live it. Too many days like this and pretty soon there will come a time when you don't get up.

Most days prior to my epiphany, I used to feel like I was in Pamplona, Spain, running with the bulls.

We are so rushed that we do things mindlessly following suggestions from everyone and everything around us. We follow directions and accept the status quo without thinking about the greater good or how we really feel about it. We follow our peer group and the trends in social media. There is so much information coming at us that we don't have time to even understand it let alone question its validity. Our world is going so fast that we go along with the masses just to survive and that includes aging. We don't have time to question how fast we are aging, or if the rate of aging around us applies to us as an individual. Most of the daily stuff is inconsequential, but moving into old age is as serious as it gets.

Who said you don't have focus? You are so focused on getting through life at light speed that you don't realize you are racing towards old age! Let's focus on living younger longer and making a dramatic change to your here and now, as well as your future. Your future you will thank-you for it.

Twenty years ago, when I realized I could control my aging and jumped off the Old Age Express I also put a stop to my mindless daily grind. I made an oath to myself that this is my life and I am going to run it my way. I didn't need anyone to tell me how old I was or what I was going to do with the years ahead. It is my life, my future and I wanted more out of life now that I wasn't overwhelmed by the stress brought about by the constant worry of running out of time.

You too have the power to change your future and I certainly hope you do.

---

BTW: Have you noticed that time slips away faster than money? Time is more valuable than money.

---

## The Advantages of Clawing Back 10 – 15 Years Now

If you are currently 50, chances are that you have been a contributing member of society for at least 30 years. Using the generally accepted idea that you will live until you are in your 80's, you have approximately another 30 years to go. This means that you have a total of 60 years of adult life of which you have 50% to go. Looking at it from this perspective instantly takes some of the pressure off, and gives you something to think about.

Using our 50 year old example, you are half way through your adult life and have probably accomplished quite a bit in the 30 years between 20 and 50. Now let's consider your retirement which is scheduled to occur in 10+ years from now followed by the last 20+ years growing older by the minute until you are a card-carrying member of the old aged strata.

*You are now part of history!*

What would an extra 10 - 15 years of productive life inserted into your timeline do for you? In simple terms you believe you are now 35 but with everything as it was a few seconds ago, except you now think and feel like a much younger you? It was mind blowing for me. Suddenly I had a computer company, a Porsche, beachside home and 30 years to build up my retirement nest egg. I also had years of hind sight and knowledge I didn't have the first time I was 35.

Money or rather lack of money was one of my biggest motivators to claw back time. If you currently earn $50,000 a year, and you had an extra 10 years of work life that would mean an extra $500,000 before tax earned during the extra 10 years you have given yourself. The figures I have used are for demonstration purposes only and do not take into consideration salary increases, promotions, retrenchments or other forms of business activity.

You would benefit even if you did something else with that, e.g. study, travel, follow your creative passions, study for a new career, spend quality time with your loved ones, contribute to your community.

Seriously, think about how you could take advantage of an extra 10 – 15 years of adult life now, instead of stressing over how you will survive your retirement in 10 years' time.

I am using very conservative numbers but what if you want to add 20 - 40 years into your life. Originally, I reset my clock from 45 back to 32 giving myself a 13 years bonus. The most interesting aspect to taking control over your aging is that not only can you reset your starting point but you also have input into your rate of aging. I reset my inner clock to 32 in 1998, it is now 2019 so you would expect that my inner clock is now 53 but surprise it is only 45. This means that I have clawed back a total of 21 years so far.

If you reset your inner clock back 10 years what great things could you accomplish?

What would this do to your decision making today? It would change your life completely.

> It's time to spend some quality time on yourself.

LIFE CYCLE BEFORE INNER CLOCK RESET

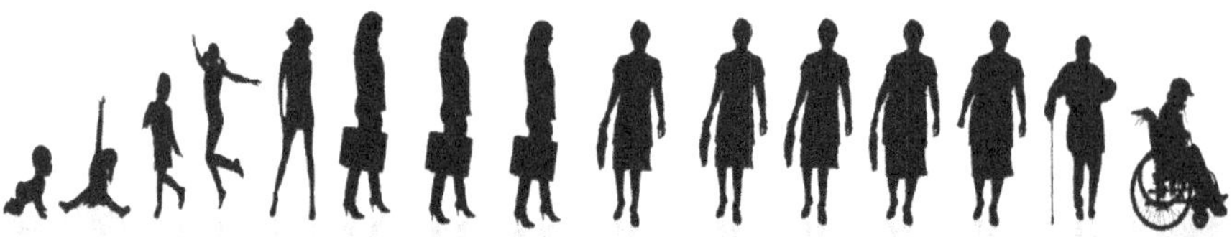

LIFE CYCLE AFTER INNER CLOCK RESET

## My Personal Outstanding Alternative to Old Age

> What does an outstanding alternative to growing old sound like, look like, feel like? Can you describe it?

When I first made the leap, I was on those fat scales looking down at a neon green sign telling me that I was clinically dead and had too much body fat. At that point, life looked really miserable. I was in my early 40s and I was thinking: 'I'm in my 40's nearly 50 and 50 means my life is almost over."

> I was tired, overweight and unhappy.

My mind made a quantum leap ahead, and suddenly I had transitioned from a miserable 45-year-old to a desperate 50. Wow, I'm now thinking as if I am already 50 which is nearly retirement, and I don't have enough money and I don't have this and I don't have that and, oh dear, the whole thing was just devastating? Talk about your life flashing before your eyes. It took literally seconds for me to look into my future stations and they did not look pretty. It looked more like a roller coaster ride into Hell.

Then just like in the movies I had the epiphany and I thought;

> 'Hang on, I don't have to ride this train. I can get off and run my own life.'

I didn't need to second guess myself. I immediately jumped off the train and never looked back. Well maybe once or twice for a few seconds.

Upon leaving the train the first and most important thing that happened to me was the feeling of hope followed by a rush of happiness through my entire body.

> It was like someone had opened all the windows and I could breathe again! I was free!

One minute, I was looking down the barrel of retirement, being broke and miserable. I changed my thinking and in a split second all the fears and stress that had been washing through my body disappeared!

The magic is I believed I could change my future and I took responsibility for it. Taking responsibility was something I was experienced at. I always took control of my life It had just never occurred to me that I could take control of aging and time.

> It's hard to believe, but I went from old to bold in 60 seconds!

That's why I call it an epiphany. Something from somewhere out there, shot this idea into my head and that was it. It was done and dusted. I then proceeded to learn methods to reinforce my thinking; to reinforce my new beliefs and to make this feeling last.

In my mind, I was now 13 years younger and had time to lose that weight and change my life. The overwhelming feeling that I was running out of time and the associated stress of aging was gone. It was incredible how much the stress of aging was controlling my life decisions. I now had the freedom to breathe instead of being in panic mode.

The epiphany gave me hope and allowed me to look forward to a future that had potential.

Suddenly I had some head space. I stepped off the fat scales and immediately started work on backing up my new beliefs about aging and time.

As I said earlier in this chapter, after I had a bit of time to get used to the idea that I was in control of my age, I also realized that I could also control the rate at which I age. These two things go hand-in-hand. It makes sense that if I can control one, I can control the other.

I knew I was on the right track, but I also knew that knowing something is true is not sufficient to make it so. Hence, I have spent many years since then studying and researching the topic of mind over matter, and how one lives younger for longer.

My new belief needed to be reinforced. I started seriously studying NLP and more recently neuroplasticity has added scientific weight to the process of rewiring one's brain.

> You've got to want it, believe it, practice it and act on it. Your brain can't rewire itself. You can't sit on your hands and think it. You have to create and implement a 'process of change'... Roselyn Poon

**So, what has happened to me since my epiphany gave me the courage to jump off the Old Age Express**?

Obviously, a lot of things changed. First of all, I stopped panicking and stressing over running out of time. I realized that I was a very fortunate young lady, and that I had years to do the things I was previously worried about, and the things I didn't even know I wanted to do.

*BTW: The real biggie for me was no longer being stressed about running out of time.*

A few years after my epiphany I closed my computer software company, packed my first life into a few storage units and left for America. I wanted to do something different. I had been a computer software developer all my life, and a chronic workaholic. Forget about smelling the roses, I ran over them to get to the future.

My Aussie girlfriends were all about the same age as me. We had regular monthly dinners, and I remember my last get together with them. The conversation went something like this:

'You've got a brilliant life. You've got a fantastic life. You should be saving up and getting ready for retirement. You will be back. Why America, they are crazy over there? Are you crazy?'

They were contented passengers on the Old Age Express, and it didn't make any sense to them that I should leave my first-class seat to wonder off into the unknown.

I had a fabulous lifestyle, but why would I want to keep doing the same thing over and over until I died? Life is not meant to be that way. I had a new life to live and I was going to do exactly that. Live it!

I remember thinking, 'I refuse to be that little mouse on the treadmill.'

So, I relocated to America and reengineered my entire view on the world. I started to do things that I enjoyed prior to entering the work force. Somewhere along the way I had forgotten about so many things that used to mean something to me. They had been replaced with technology, fast cars, and designer suits. You don't have to be a man to fall into this lifestyle.

Personal story: When I was a young teenager I often designed and sewed my own clothes. I saved and bought pieces of fabric from the odds and ends basket. I could never afford to buy zips or patterns. I would lay the fabric out on my bedroom floor and draw the outline of my pattern pieces with a pen.

My mother didn't sew but for some reason she had an old Singer sewing machine. I didn't realize at the time that I was poor. I was focused on designing and making my clothes the way I imagined them.

By the end of my teens I entered the fledgling IT industry and instantly forgot all about sewing and other artistic pursuits until I reset my inner clock.

A few years ago, my life partner Bunker Bradley and I, started a unique women's fashion company. The joy and excitement of seeing something materialize from a drawing is just as exciting today as it was when I was sitting on my bedroom floor a lifetime ago.

BTW: Our couture garments don't have zips or snaps either.

---

I have done all sorts of things since coming to America. I remember when I was in Australia and newly married, my now ex-husband Peter bought a Nikon SLR. I loved that camera and we shared it. My passion was macro photography and I would spend hours taking photographs of the beautiful fuchsias growing in our garden. When we divorced, Peter took the camera equipment and I forgot about photography.

A lifetime later in Las Vegas I am not referred to as the Porsche racing driver and computer geek, but as the fashion designer and photographer. Who would have predicted this? Certainly not me.

Roselyn signing autographs before a Porsche race in Australia

Who would have thought that when I reprogrammed my thinking to reset my internal clock, I would return to my youthful endeavors of photography and fashion? For an entire lifetime these passions lay dormant but now I have the time and the youthful enthusiasm to give them a go.

At the start, I didn't have a detailed plan for my future other than breathing and improving my old age prospects by delaying it. I had a lot of experiences to help me work out what I didn't want to do, and thanks to my epiphany I now had a lot of time to experiment.

> Inserting 10 – 20 years into your timeline now, gives you a chance to breathe and evaluate your life, without the stress of worrying about time.

I really wanted to get off that treadmill and look around. I had been working non-stop, going from one goal to the next without a breath for most of my life. The one thing that I was sure about was that I wanted to write a book to make people aware that they too can reset their inner clock, and get valuable years back into their life. I still wanted to make enough money to maintain a lifestyle that would sustain me during retirement, but guess what?

I have decided not to retire. ... Roselyn

Claw back 10 years, release the stress and you may even benefit biologically too.

If you are always in a hurry, your biological clock speeds up. If you feel you have all the time in the world, your biological clock slows down.... Deepak Chopra – Grow Younger Live Longer

## Your Personal Outstanding Alternative to Old Age

You can't sit down on a Sunday afternoon and say, my future's going to be this or that. Well, sorry, you can do, however be warned it may change over time. You are evolving and experiencing your world through the mindset of a younger more enthusiastic you so obviously your thoughts and plans will evolve too.

Ask yourself; "What's the one thing that I really would love to do or desperately avoid?"

That's how the process started for me. I knew what I passionately wanted to avoid a poor, lonely miserable retirement.

This is your chance to insert 10 – 20 years into your future and change it for the better. Take your time. You have time on your side so make the best of it.

This is your life and you get to choose if you stay on the Old Age Express or jump off and take control before it is too late.

I encourage you to jump off the Old Age Express, and take responsibility for creating your own future story. Consider this point in time as intermission or half time, and everyone knows the second half is always much more exciting than the first.

Most of us accept the fact that one day we're going to die, and I have yet to come across anyone who has found an alternative. It is also hard to argue with the saying that death and taxes are the only two definite happenings in our lives. However, we know there are many ways to optimize our taxes and surprisingly there is a variety of ways to cheat old age and possible defer death to a later date. It starts with resetting your inner clock.

*All alternatives end in death; however, it is how you get there that counts. ... Roselyn*

I can't tell you what your alternatives are. My job is to make you aware that you have alternatives to spending a third of your life in old age.

**Start Brainstorming Your Amazing Alternative to Old Age**

The following is a warm up exercise to help get you in to the right state of mind for living younger longer.

**Time for you to do some work:**

Sit back and relax. Try to slow down your mind. This is a deliberate fantasy moment. It doesn't have to have anything to do with reality. This will start up your mental engine.

Ask yourself, if I had an extra 10, 15 or 20 years now:

How would I feel about life?

How would I feel in general?

What problems and issues could I attend to and maybe fix?

What are the kinds of things that I would love to do?

What would I do first?

If I had all the time in the world, what would I really be doing right now?

What could I do for my family, friends, community or the world?

If you had some difficulty with this exercise, I suggest getting physical. Go to the gym, bake a cake, or the best option is going for a walk. You need to do some mindless activity so that the noise in your head quietens down. Let it go for now, however give yourself a goal of coming up with at least one response to any one of the questions each day. This will take the pressure off.

Personally, I find the best way to come up with any kind of meaningful response to a question that requires some pretty deep diving is to set myself the task of creating a list with 20 responses. The first 10 entries are usually fairly easy. However, it then gets progressively harder. I leave it for a couple of days but leave the list in plain view. After a couple of days, I find that I have managed to add another five entries. The last five entries always take me forever because now I am digging deep and mining the subconscious. The number 20 is magical because invariably the 20$^{th}$ entry is the most important one, the moneymaker. The point is to get to that magical answer, you have to ask 20 questions or give 20 answers. Number 20 is your destiny if you take up the challenge!

I want to help you find your alternative but I can't do it for you. My first boss gave me some sage advice when he said there is no such thing as a free lunch. You are going to have to dig deep and do some work but isn't a more youthful and happy state of mind and future worth it?

> Resetting your clock gives you the opportunity for a do-over if that is what you want.

## Creating Your Big Enough Why

Your WHY is comprised of two key components:

- The PAINFUL events you want to avoid
- The PLEASURABLE events you want to enjoy.

My personal two components were:

- The PAIN of being broke, and unable to enjoy my retirement.
- The PLEASURE of getting back my youthful enthusiasm for life, never retiring and deferring old age to the bitter end.

There's no point in you going through the process of working out how to get back five, 10, 15, 20 years of your life, if you don't have a good enough reason why you want those years back. Without the big WHY you will eventually falter and slip back into your old ways.

This book is about making you aware that you do not have to age in accordance with what your society considers normal. You have options!

Maybe your 'why' is to capture missed opportunities, travel more, reconcile with family members, build a bigger retirement nest egg, become closer with friends or pursue further education. Having a big enough 'why' makes all the difference in getting your years back, and moving your timeline beyond society's norm, because it keeps you moving forward. At first my why was primarily the fear of becoming a lonely old woman living on social security. I am happy to report that over the past 20 years my why has evolved with me and life is wonderful as is my future.

Over the next few days I want you to have a serious go at the following exercises. You may surprise yourself.

You should do this exercise annually to keep on track, bearing in mind that you are free to change your journey at any time.

**Time for you to do some work:**

This exercise is different to the previous one in that this time I want you to imagine what is realistically possible if you reframe your beliefs about aging and your timeline.

Ask yourself the following questions based on having an extra 10, 15 or 20 years inserted into your timeline now:

How would I feel about life?

How do I feel about the future?

How would I feel personally?

What problems and issues could I attend to and maybe fix? How does this make me feel?

What would I do first? Why would I do this first? How does it make me feel being able to do this?

What am I going to do that I missed out on earlier in my life?

What risks am I going to consider now that I have the time?

What am I going to do differently now that I am 10 – 20 years younger?

What aspects about my life would I change and why?

What are the kinds of things that I would love to do?

How do I feel knowing that there are so many things that I would like to change and new things I would like to do?

Are these feelings and plans worth the effort to reframe my beliefs about aging and time? If not, why not?

What is my alternative to resetting my inner clock and taking back time?

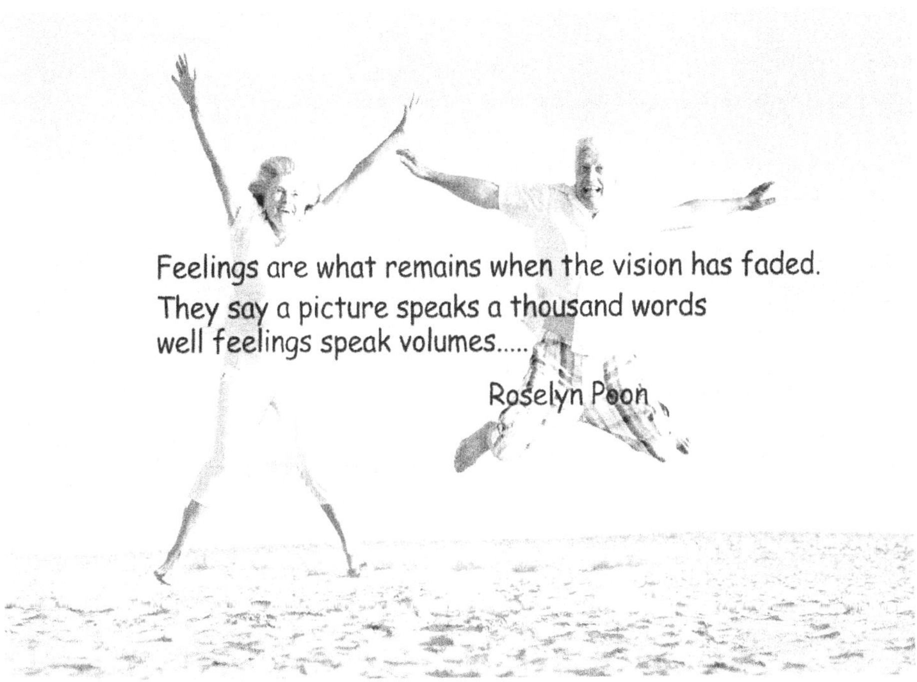

**Time for you to do some more work:**

This exercise is about feelings. Visualize each moment and feel the difference in your mind and body - remember these feelings.

**Tap into your memory banks and re-experience the following moments:**

Feeling alive with hope. If you have never felt hopeful do your best to imagine what it might feel like, or ask someone if they can explain the feeling to you.

What are your favorite moments from your past? How did you feel? Can you remember how you felt?

Think of an occasion that you remember as being special in your youth. Is there a special Birthday or Christmas morning that made you happy? How did you feel?

Recall and feel the joy of a special family event or a friend's party.
Perhaps, vacations with your children were very memorable.

You may have a great accomplishment that you are proud of and it makes you feel special. Linger on the feelings and remember this.

Think of a special lover or partner or a romantic evening that was special. What were your feelings then?

Recall happy moments during your school days.

Remember the feeling of being 25 years old again-the hope-the sparkle in your eye-the anticipation of things to come.

How do you feel after having completed such a touchy, feely exercise? Did you notice your body posture and breathing changing? Is your mind floating with anticipation of what the future could be with a more hopeful and enthusiastic mind set?

Comparing today's feelings and thoughts about a subject or something you have always wanted to do, or be, with those you had 20 years ago is a quick way to know if age is holding you back. If today's feelings are tinged with sadness, and regret that you missed the boat and no longer have enough time, then add these feelings to your WHY. Remember your why is made up of pain and pleasure.

BTW: If you genuinely cannot come up with a big enough why to give believing you are younger a fair go, then that's cool. It is your life and I am an advocate of people taking charge of their own lives.

Your next exercise is to close the book and go back to what you were doing before you opened it. Thank-you for getting this far and I wish you well. If you ever change your mind you know where to find us.

What would life be like living your real purpose with 20 years inserted into your time line? You could be 40 or 60 or 90, the starting point is irrelevant. It's your state of mind that counts. What will your new future be like? What will tomorrow be like?

BTW: I don't expect you to be able to design your incredible alternative in any great detail right this minute. That's really not possible, but what is possible, though, is to decide that you want to bring back those feelings of hope and being alive knowing you are working on getting time back.

Your new adventure is like starting a new business. Most new business ventures take about five years to really get some critical mass. During which time you have to get up every day and keep going. Keep reminding yourself you've got time; you're doing everything right. The great thing about this time is that you are not starting from scratch. You have amassed a great deal of experience and are much wiser than you were 20 years ago.

BTW: You have the incredible benefit of hindsight.

Now, thanks to your newly discovered awareness, you have the chance to make a conscious decision to reset your inner clock and add valuable years and life to your lifetime.

Most people think that growing old is inevitable and it is, however most of us speed up the process and provide little to no resistance. You are about to slow it down. Pay attention to your health, diet, stress, activity levels and most importantly your state-of-mind.

**Control your own destiny by controlling your state-of-mind.**

---

BTW: My 20th entry is to live an active meaningful life until the end which is currently 120. I've re-invented myself and challenge myself every day. I'm doing things that at first, I knew nothing about, but knowing that time is on my side, I pushed through the fear and with each challenge made my world a little bigger and brighter.

---

BTW: Current estimates put the figure of total centenarians worldwide at about 450,000. In total numbers the United States has the most centenarians with current estimates as high as 72,000.

Japan is second to the US, with a current population of about 30,000. However, that number has almost quadrupled in the last 10 years, making the centenarians population in Japan rising more dramatically than anywhere else. At its current rate of expansion Japan's population of centenarians may rival that of the United States in sheer numbers in the years ahead. Certainly by 2050 Japan proportionally will have the most centenarians in the world.

...... website TheCentenarian.co.uk

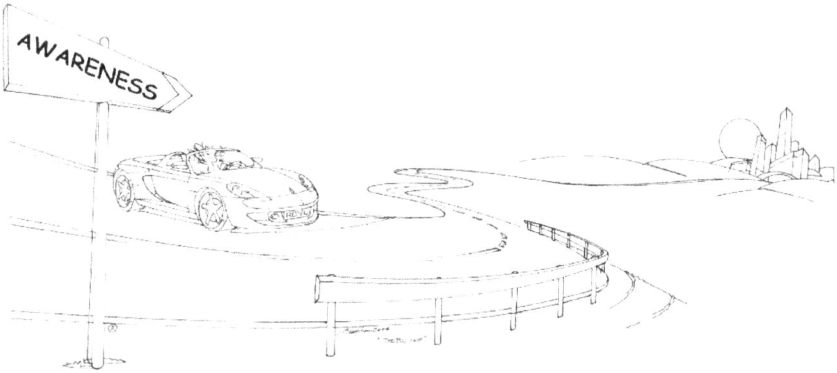


Drawing by Bunker Bradley

**Next:** Awareness is the beginning of your journey, and with it comes change.

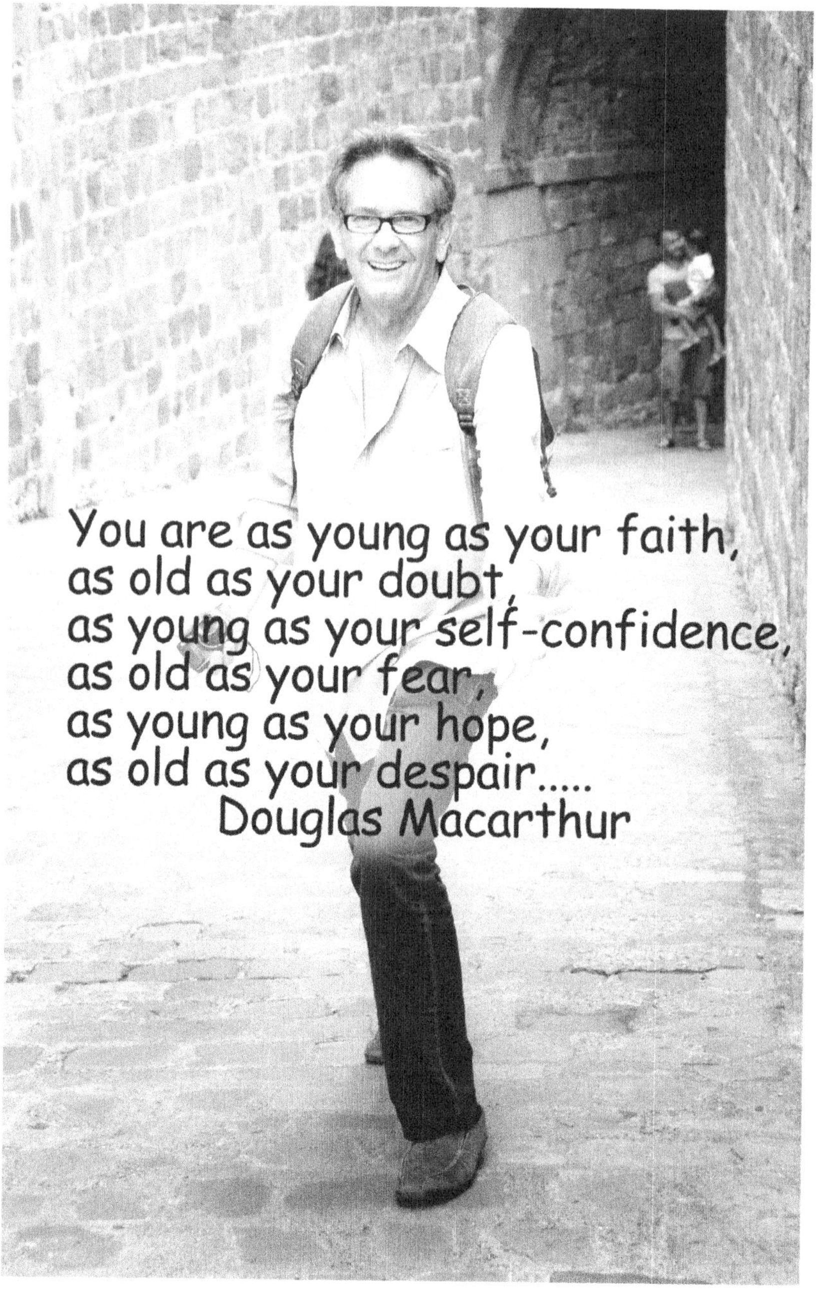
You are as young as your faith,
as old as your doubt,
as young as your self-confidence,
as old as your fear,
as young as your hope,
as old as your despair.....
Douglas Macarthur

# Chapter 5

## The Power of Beliefs

> Believing you can take control of your aging is the first step to taking charge of your future.

I have devoted this chapter to introducing you to the power your beliefs have over your life. Later in the book we discuss your beliefs regarding time and aging, however we must first get a basic understanding of how beliefs work. The more you are able to understand how beliefs work the easier it will be for you to reprogram your beliefs to live younger longer. Your beliefs are the reason why you are aging at the rate you are and more importantly, updated beliefs on aging will help you to get that extra 10 - 20 years inserted into your timeline.

Your beliefs regarding aging affect your state of mind and how old or young you feel. They are the cause of the Premature Aging Virus and after some upgrading, they are also the cure.

If you genuinely believe you are 20 years younger than your age according to your driver's license, more than likely you are a very happy camper. On the other hand, if you conform to the stereotypical description of aging as per your environment, you are probably stressed over growing older every day and running out of time. You are probably making decisions based on scarcity rather than abundance.

Let's look at the definition of the word belief from the website www.dictionary.com.

Noun:
1. Something believed; an opinion or conviction
2. Confidence in the truth or existence of something not immediately susceptible to rigorous proof
3. Confidence; faith; trust
4. A religious tenet or tenet; religious creed or faith.

Notice that a belief is something believed and not susceptible to rigorous proof. This means it doesn't have to be supported by tangible proof.

**Why are beliefs so important?**

> Your beliefs create your world and your reality. You are what you believe – albeit good or *bad*.

Beliefs influence your responses to, and feelings about your world. They influence your expectations about the future and your memories of the past. Beliefs are your interface to the rest of the world. Just as you are unique, your belief interface is unique to you.

Beliefs are the basis for everything you say and do in life. Most of the time you won't even be aware that beliefs are operating and influencing you. This is because over time, they have become a fully integrated part of your sub-conscious. Beliefs run on auto-pilot for the most part unless challenged.

Think about the concept for a minute. You have beliefs about:

- Yourself
- Your friends
- Your family
- The next door neighbors
- Politics
- Religion
- Culture
- Music
- Ecology
- Environment
- Children
- Driving
- Food
- Exercise
- Study
- Work
- Money

The list goes on forever.

Your belief system affects your decision making and contributes to your personality and psyche. Think of your beliefs as a filter or more accurately as an interpreter. Your beliefs translate your experiences for your mind.

Let's look at examples of some of these beliefs and how they work:

- If you believe that you are boring and have nothing of interest to say to people, you will avoid interacting with people on every level. This will affect your childhood, teenage years and even the type of career you pursue.
- If you believe that a friend is someone who will never let you down, you will rely on the support of your friends and you will most certainly never let a friend down.
- If you believe that your children will develop into good people if you spend quality time with them more so than giving them things to keep them amused, you will make sure that your career does not consume every waking moment of your life and you will make time for your children.
- If you believe that your neighbor is weird, you will avoid contacting them and probably make sure that you go to your letter box at a different time to when your neighbor goes to theirs.
- If you believe that you have to earn every dollar you have, you will probably not buy lotto tickets, or gamble, and you will stay in a situation whereby your income is directly dependent upon the number of hours you work.

> Beliefs are like breathing, we don't worry or think about it until we have asthma or under stress.... Merryn Armstrong-Poon

**Your beliefs create your reality**

Beliefs allow us to go through life without having to question everything and make thousands of decisions every day, however, it's really a mind trip. We may not be seeing and experiencing reality in accordance with the people around us, but it is our reality and that is what matters.

I have a friend whose passion is motor bike racing. He can't understand why I am happy to be a racing driver but not willing to race a motor bike. To him they are the same thing but not to me. The following is a list of my beliefs regarding motor bike racing.

- Only crazy people race motor bikes
- Seriously dangerous
- Everyone ends up in hospital sooner or later and often on multiple occasions
- Super human skill level is required
- Some of the cornering seems to defy physics
- The riders are masters at balance and fearless
- Great spectator sport
- Young man's sport

Can you imagine me actually taking up motor cycle racing with this set of beliefs? Not likely.

All of the comments listed above are things I believe to be true about the sport of motor bike racing. He sees motorbike racing through a completely different set of beliefs which allows him to see it as fun, exciting, safe and a great way to spend his free time.

**Time for you to do some work:**

What sports do you play or avoid like the plague?

List your beliefs about these sports.

This simple exercise will introduce you to the act of analyzing your beliefs. Even if you don't like sports you can list your beliefs about sports.

**Beliefs come in all shapes and sizes**

There are two primary belief categories:

- Core beliefs are the very essence of how you see yourself, other people, the world, and the future. Your core beliefs are your bench mark for your response to your interaction with the world around you. For example, if you believe loyalty is a key element to being a good person you will very likely be a very loyal friend to have around. You will find it hard to believe that people can be treacherous and disloyal.

The simplest analogy to describe a core belief is the old question: are you a half glass full or half empty person?

Examples of core beliefs are:

- Loyalty
- Commitment
- Open-mindedness
- Honesty
- Compassion
- Spirit of adventure
- Positivity
- Optimism
- Passion
- Courage
- Patriotism
- Service to others
- Environmentalism

- Regular belief is the label I use for beliefs that have developed and morphed over time. They are a result of your interaction with your world.

  Examples of regular beliefs are:

  - Smoking causes cancer
  - Takes money to make money
  - Gambling is a loser's game
  - The people next door are weird

There are also different types of beliefs, for example:

- Limiting beliefs – these hold you back. Example:
  - You believe that you are not smart enough to apply for a university position so you never try.
  - You believe that no matter how hard you work you will never get promoted, so you put in just enough effort to ensure you don't get fired.

- Toxic beliefs – these poison your thinking and create havoc. Example:
  - You believe that people can't be trusted which makes you suspicious and jealous when you are in a relationship.

- You believe that you are obese even though your doctor tells you that you are starving yourself to death.

- Empowering beliefs – these are the best kind of beliefs. They inspire and encourage you to keep growing and experience the world around you. Example:

  - Your belief that persistency wins in the end gives you the willpower and fortitude to keep going in the face of adversity. Persistency was obviously Edison's motto. When he was asked about his multiple attempts to perfect the light bulb, he responded: I have not failed. I've just found 10,000 ways that won't work."
  - Your belief that there is a lesson to be learned in every outcome helps to keep you moving ahead even when you have made a few wrong turns.

---

BTW: If you believe that you cannot lose weight then you will not lose weight. It is nearly impossible to act in discordance with your beliefs. You may wish and want to lose weight and you may even fully understand what it takes for you to lose weight, but deep down you believe that you will never lose weight, and beliefs are self-fulfilling so you will never lose weight while that limiting belief is in force.

---

## The Difference Between Thoughts and Beliefs

Thoughts are things that happen constantly throughout the day. Thoughts are transient. You can see them, look at them, and a lot of times you will simply dismiss them. Thoughts are not a subconscious activity; they reside temporarily in your conscious mind.

Example:" What's the weather like today?", "I shouldn't be wearing this short dress".

The issue I have with thoughts, is that you need to be aware that a thought which is brought to mind regularly, could become a belief. As they say be careful what you think about because it could become a reality.

Unlike core beliefs, thoughts have minimal long-term effect on your actions or your state of mind. A core belief is a thought that has undergone scrutiny, questioning, and accepted by you as true and binding, at which point the thought has been transformed into a belief. Remember a belief does not have to stand up to someone else's scrutiny. Once it becomes a core belief it has input into everything you say and do from that point forwards. A thought however is transient, it is something that you do not necessarily believe or even notice. You have as many thoughts in a day as there are commuters driving to work in the morning.

*Come to think of it, you probably have lots of thoughts about your fellow commuters, but in the majority of cases you don't act on those thoughts; or rather I hope not.*

Thoughts pop in and out of your mind constantly. Fortunately, most thoughts speed through your mind without even the slightest acknowledgment by you which is great because it is the only way we are able to get anything done. However, at any point in time we can slow our thought processing down and investigate a thought if it catches our attention, or we can speed up our awareness to catch a thought.

You can even read and understand things without turning them into beliefs. Try the following thought exercise. Read through the following list and notice that as soon as you read a statement, thoughts comprised of pictures, sounds and sensations just pop into your head. They may not even be related to the statement you just read, but triggered by the statement. Also notice what happens when you read a statement that connects with something you believe in or strongly oppose.

- Lactose free milk, easy to digest.
- American Airlines Miami to Las Vegas daily nonstop.
- Women of all ages love flowers.
- The bigger the toys the smaller the boys.
- It's too nice a day to be stuck in the office.
- Going to the right college is everything.
- Technology is taking over the world.

A belief is something that you hold to be true and consequently it has a direct effect on your attitudes and actions. Some of your beliefs will be common and some quite particular to you. The following is a list of common beliefs:

- Humans cannot fly unassisted.
- Water naturally runs downhill.

- Kindness is rewarded by kindness.
- 1 + 1 = 2
- People are basically honest.
- Smoking causes cancer.
- Money doesn't grow on trees.
- Exercise is good for me.
- I can drive home after drinking.
- I can leave my home unlocked because I live in the country.
- I must work hard for every cent.
- Only fools buy lottery tickets.
- I am not worthy
- I am not good enough
- Sex before marriage is a sin
- Skinny French fries are better than chunky fries

It is feasible to believe and even know that something is factual without it becoming one of your governing beliefs. I know that eating French fries will not help me to lose weight, but it doesn't stop me from eating them. Why? It is because I have a more powerful belief that a handful of fries won't have any effect on my weight.

---

BTW: *Isn't this the type of logic cigarette smokers use? Yes, smoking causes cancer but not in my case, I am one of the lucky ones.*

---

What about people who buy lottery tickets even though they have been told time and time again that the chances are 1 in a billion as proven by technology, however they have a stronger belief that someone has to win so why not them.

Thoughts are light, superficial and race along the surface of your mind. If by simply having a thought about being thin actually changed our eating and exercising regime, the multi-billion-dollar diet industry would fold up before lunchtime. How many of us have read the promise on the cover of a magazine, immediately purchased it thinking this is great, I will be 10 lbs. lighter by Sunday. However, we never even read the article when we get home, we just flicked through it and dropped it onto the top of the stack. If thoughts were powerful, we would have been 10 lbs. lighter by just reading the cover, and we would never have even had to buy the magazine. However, some of you would have read the cover and it created a thought that caught your attention. Having caught your attention, you investigated it further and if after several layers of interrogation and evaluation by you, you truly accepted the beliefs necessary to make the diet program work; you would lose the 10lbs.

To recap, thoughts are fleeting and superficial hence they have very limited long-lasting power over your state of mind or being.

> Thoughts are like the mist.

However, a thought can become a belief if it is repeated often enough with conviction. Eventually that thought, be it good or bad, will become automatic and transition to a belief stored in your subconscious.

> 'The mind is everything. What you think, you become'.... Buddha

**How beliefs are created**

Beliefs originate from your environment, parents, teachers, friends, colleagues, the media, associates, travel, study, role models, your own preferences and dominant state of mind. Just about everything and everywhere has the potential to create or enforce a belief. Someone you look up to may say they believe aliens are living amongst us here on Earth. They present their case for their belief and because of your respect for their intelligence, you could decide that it sounds plausible so you too will become a believer in aliens living in your neighborhood.

> Everything you are today and will be tomorrow is a direct result of your beliefs... Roselyn

It is important to remember that beliefs do not have to be supported by hard facts. They can be created by your sheer will and determination to believe. A large number of our beliefs are the result of listening to someone else, following the herd, accepting what is said in the media without personal research and validation. Beliefs are things that we chose to believe and follow, and once we have decided to believe we actively consciously and sub-consciously seek reinforcement.

We humans don't like thinking that we are in the wrong so very often we will unconsciously seek evidence to support our beliefs. Harking back to my belief that smoking causes cancer, I don't ever remember coming across an article that disputed my belief even though it was hotly debated by the medical profession and reported by the press in the 1960's. I only ever saw the affirmative.

---

BTW: My father often said that I only saw what I wanted to see.

---

We re-affirm our beliefs constantly throughout the day without being consciously aware that we are doing this, e.g. when you are stopped at a red traffic light you immediately berate yourself for always getting red lights; you catch sight of someone who is trim and looks great in their clothes and your inner voice says I will never look like that person I just don't have the genes or the will power etc.

A belief started out as a thought that caught your attention. Once on your radar, you researched it and validated it to the point that you firmly believed in the thought and incorporated it into your library of beliefs, or disregarded it and relegated it back to a mere thought.

A thought can also convert to a belief simply through being exposed to it repeatedly. Eventually it becomes familiar. Other means of validating a thought are wanting and wishing it to be true, confirmation by a higher authority or masses, and vividness of backup information. Brain washing can also convert thoughts into beliefs.

Examples of beliefs you may have held true when you were a child are the "Tooth Fairy", "Easter Bunny" and "Santa Clause". All of these beliefs have since been proven to you to be folklore and dropped however, when you were small you parents told you they were true and subsequent events proved that to be the case, i.e. Easter eggs appeared, money appeared and your tooth disappeared, gifts from Santa Clause appeared on Christmas morning and the cookies and milk were gone, quid pro quo they must exist.

---

Oh, and add to this that we wanted them to exist and our peer group also wanted to believe.

---

We have to have reasons, explanations and even rationalizations to believe, however the reasons do not have to be true or real so long as they feel right and true to us.

Like a lot of women, I have grown up wishing my legs were six inches longer because I believed that my weight was better suited to someone taller. It started when my first boyfriend asked me to lose weight for his 18th birthday party. Until that time, I knew I wasn't as skinny as my girl-friends but I wasn't worried about it. However, from the moment my boyfriend put the notion into my head that I needed to lose weight, I believed that I was over-weight regardless. This belief remained with me for decades, even though when I checked with medical weight to age tables I was always in the average weight for age bracket.

---

Somehow my beliefs interpreted the tables to suit themselves.

---

I remember going to the famous diet clinic Jenny Craig a few months before my wedding, and the consultant was horrified that I was 132 lbs. Looking back I realized that I was never over weight, but my belief that I was overweight was controlling my experiences. Even when I dropped down to 105 lbs. for my boyfriend, it never occurred to me to think of myself as skinny. It wasn't until I started a women's fashion company much later in life that I re-evaluated my belief about my weight.

My current belief is that I am ok and I keep an eye on the healthy side of things like cholesterol and blood pressure so that I can benefit from my extra years. The point is that I lived with that limiting belief that I was over weight for more than 40 years. I allowed a boyfriend to label me and I believed it without giving it a second thought. That misbelief dictated what I wore and how I felt about myself every day of my life in spite of the compliments I would receive from people around me who saw a healthy, happy woman with a great shape.

---

Beliefs are very personal and not black and white.

---

'Wow I lost a pound, and I look and feel fantastic!'

**Beliefs Are Your Colored Glasses**

It is true what they say about rose-colored glasses. I was in Hawaii a couple of years ago and I bought a pair of wonderful rose-colored sun glasses. In my defense all I can say is that I grew up in the hippie era. Remember when psychedelic was the in word and multi colored sun glasses were a must. It was a bit overcast the day I bought these rose-colored glasses and sure enough as soon as I put them on the world truly looked happier and much brighter. Obviously, the physical scenery hadn't changed but the glasses had changed the representation of the scene in my mind's eye, and that set off a chain of other changes within me.

For example, certain elements of the scene that were subdued became highlighted by the color, the sky looked brighter and my physiology changed accordingly. The filter between it and my brain had changed. Try it for yourself the next time you come across a sunglass vendor at the mall. Live dangerously and try on a pair of rose-colored glasses. They are back in fashion so it is your chance to be cool again and carry out an experiment at the same time. Beliefs are a little like our colored glasses, except they are a multi colored disk continually spinning around in our head and in front of our eyes and even in our ears.

Sometimes you are wearing rose colored glasses and then a minute later you swap them for clear or gray. The other interesting aspect is that a person standing next to you wearing different colored glasses will see the same scene differently.

Another great example of the power of belief is listening to peoples' contradicting opinions on an accident. A simple "rear-ender" can be viewed by a passing driver as the fault of the person in front because they stopped too quickly whereas, another driver may think that it was the rear driver's fault because he braked too late.

Either view does not change the fact that the accident occurred.

It is the old question "Is the glass half full or half empty?" The answer depends on your beliefs.

**Here is a great example of a real person's set beliefs**

To help you understand a little more about how beliefs affect every part of your life, a very dear friend agreed to share her beliefs with us. The following are her beliefs as at 15 years ago. I make mention on the timing as a person's beliefs can change over time. Merryn has given me permission to use her list.

<u>Merryn – typical single mother of three young adult children</u>

- It is hard to list my own beliefs because they are not things I consciously think about.
- Everything I do is based on a belief.
- Breathing is like beliefs – we don't worry or think about it until we have asthma or under stress.
- What Merryn believes about herself:
  - I believe that the past is what has made me who I am today.
  - I believe I am an average person.
  - I believe I am a good mum.
  - I believe that I am not the sort of person who will change the world.
  - I believe that I am more independent now than I was before.
  - I believe that I may lose my independence in exchange for a new partner.
  - I believe that it is a possibility that when my children marry and create a life of their own, they will no longer need me and not include me in their lives.

- I believe that I will not be able to live independently after retirement even though I have my own home and a pension income. I believe that it won't be enough with the way cost of living has increased in my lifetime alone.
- I follow my parents' beliefs: work hard 9-5, have kids, own your own home, stay married.
- Try not to think about the future because the future is all about the next pay packet and paying the bills and buying food.
- I believe most self-help books are written for robots rather than people.
- I don't want to be "up there" because it is stress land – I cope with enough stress with my middleclass life. I believe you have to prove yourself day in and day out – taking on extra responsibilities. No attraction to me at all. It is not that I can't do it, I just don't want to do it.
- I believe that changing beliefs will not happen overnight – it will take repetition over a period of time.

- Merryn's view regarding aging and the passing of time:
  - I used to think 40 was so old but now that I am here, it isn't.
  - When I was 20, 40 wasn't even on my radar.
  - I don't have any thoughts regarding 70 because I don't think about the future. My future extends to my next pay packet.
  - When I think back over my life the first thought that comes to mind is how quickly it has gone.
  - When you think ahead it seems like forever away – too far away to relate to.
  - I believe that I don't have to worry about the future because it is miles away.
  - People go through life sub-consciously – not aware of time slipping by.
  - My recent vacation – before I came away, I thought 3 weeks was forever, I believed that I would miss the kids, my friends were worried about what they would do without me, however after 2 weeks away the time has flown by. Why is that?
  - Remember how long an hour feels when you are doing something you like as compared to something you hate. Like a date that went for a week but in actual fact it was an evening.
  - 60 is old – given that you made me think about it.

- Old means the end of or near the end of my working life, no longer partying and going out to bars, hanging out with friends, drinking and dancing. Tea and coffee, have tea at 5pm and going to bed at 7pm.
- At 20, 40 seemed old, but now at 40, I still feel young and 60 seems old – the question is what am I going to feel like at 60, hopefully I am going to feel young and 80 is old.
- We think of our parents at that age and it seems old.
- I don't believe I will get to 80 because my parents both died early in their 60's and I already have diabetes.
- The only thing that would inspire me to live younger longer is so that I can have active time with my grandchildren. I don't want to be an invalid grandparent!!
- I want to live younger longer to maintain my independence.

- What Merryn believes about her children:
  - I believe child number one is a worker and a doer he will always work, I believe he will not have his own family until 30, I think he follows my beliefs, work, pay the bills and try to lead an honest life. He is an honest hard worker with no great potential to be wealthy – just comfortable and happy.
  - I believe child number two will get married settle down and have kids. She will always be a worker with other people. Smartest out of the 3 of them academically smart with people skills. She plans more than the rest of them.
  - I think child number three is an ideas' person. He is the one who is going to be looking for the new and unusual. Honest and caring. He has personality – he could be a gourmet chief with own TV show to a comedian – whatever he will do will be in the public eye – he is the people person.
  - Their belief that they need to work to live comes from me.

Thank-you Merryn

**Time for you to do some work:**

List 20 things you believe about yourself.

List 20 things you believe about your life thus far.

List 20 things you believe about your future.

List 20 things you believe in?

## Beliefs Are Bigger Than You and Me

Beliefs are all powerful and not limited to individuals like you and me.

Common beliefs can be held by:

- A family
- A group of friends
- A community
- A special interest group
- An entire country
- A small number of people
- An enormous number of people.

A single belief can exert power over an entire country and even the world. One of the best examples of a non-religious based powerful belief that affected our entire planet is the 4-minute mile barrier for sprinters.

It was widely believed that man was not physically capable of running a mile in 4 minutes. This belief stopped thousands of runners from believing they could break the 4-minute barrier until May 6 1954 when Roger Bannister did exactly that.

In the following years athletes trained believing that they could break the 4-minute barrier and did so regularly. As at 2018, Hicham El Guerrouj is the current men's record holder with his time of 3:43.13 mins, and Svetlana Masterkova has the women's record of 4:12.56 mins.

All it took was one person to destroy a globally accepted belief.

There are many beliefs held by entire groups and cultures for example:

- The Australian aborigines have a powerful belief called 'pointing the bone'. Even in modern times the Aborigines believe that this legend is responsible for a number of tribal deaths. In simple terms a human or emu bone is fashioned into a needle shape approximately 6 to 9 inches in length with hair pasted to one end with sap. Appointed killers from the tribe are given the bone, and the task of hunting down the doomed tribal member. It is their job to condemn him or her to death by kneeling and pointing the bone at them.

  Apparently, death usually follows within four to five days. The practice is still common enough in the Australian outback that local hospitals and nursing staff are trained to manage illness caused by "bad spirits" and bone pointing.

---

Not All Beliefs Are Born Equal ... Roselyn

---

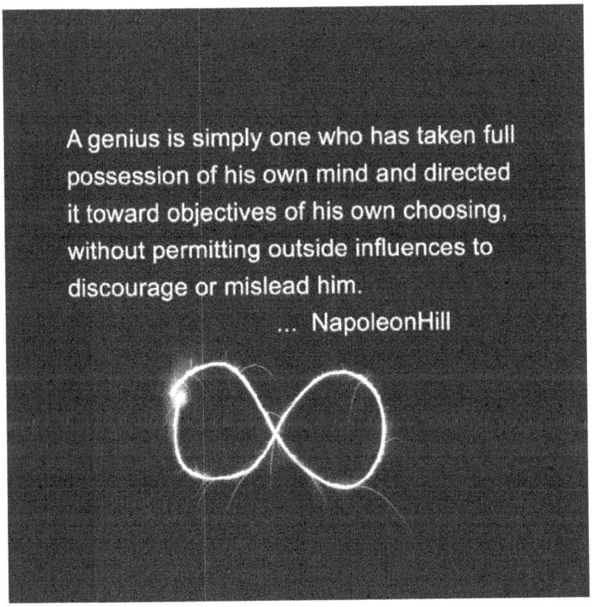

## Belief Hierarchy

There is also a hierarchy of beliefs, meaning some beliefs have more influence over your mind than others. Example:

- I keep worrying about dieting however I never really go on a diet for more than 4 hours. I believe that this is because my highest belief in this matter is that I am not fat.
- I have another belief that carbs especially chocolate and ice cream are not good for me but I seem to eat them anyway, albeit in small doses. This is because my higher belief is that everything in moderation is ok.

I know it reads like I am trying to justify my actions however it is the truth of the matter. One belief has more weight with me than another, no pun intended.

Do you have a behavior you wish you could change but for some unknown reason you haven't been able to? If you do, I would like you to see if you can uncover the more powerful belief that is stopping your from changing. Uncovering the higher belief will allow you to work out which belief needs reframing or at least you will know why you are seemingly failing at what you think you want to do.

**Time for you to do some work:**

Create a list of at least 3 habits that you would love to change but so far you have had little to no success. List your thoughts and beliefs about each habit.

During this process, the most important thing to do is ask yourself if you have any beliefs that seem to be in opposition to your wishes.

There is a very good chance that you will uncover opposing beliefs that are higher up in your belief hierarchy, and these beliefs are stopping you from changing the habits you want to change.

The next step is to decide which beliefs you want to keep and which ones need to be removed or down-graded.

In other words, you need to re-evaluate what is more important to you with regards to these habits you thought you wanted to change. You may well be very surprised.

The true secret to living a wonderful life and becoming the best person we can be, lies in our belief system.

## Belief Life Cycle and Change

As we discussed earlier, thoughts repeated with emotion may be come beliefs stored in your subconscious. Once you have accepted a belief it is very rare to revisit or question it. In fact, on occasion we will defend it to the death, even if during the battle we start to see the other person's point of view.

Later in this section you may be waging war against yourself. You will be questioning your long-held beliefs regarding old age, aging, and your ability to reclaim 10 – 20 years of your life.

It is the simple act of accept and forget that allows the premature aging virus to kill years of your life but it is also this process that we are going to use to reclaim those years. It is important to understand that even though beliefs are central to your being, you can change them. Change can happen naturally as you move through your life or on occasion questions are raised which help you to become aware of some of your beliefs that no longer serve you, and need to be reviewed. Case in point are your beliefs regarding time and aging.

Sometimes you grow out of a belief quite naturally because you and or your environment changes.

Personal story: When I was little, I believed in Santa Clause because the people around me assured me he was real. I could see him on TV, and I even sat on his knee. My grandma would help me write a letter each year and we would walk to the postbox and mail it to the North Pole. If that wasn't enough proof, I even had my photo taken with him at one of the large department stores in Melbourne. I believed so much that when we left that department store to cross the street and visit him again on the roof top of another store, and I looked up as we crossed the street to see if I could see him flying over from store to store. Over time, people around me stopped reassuring me that Santa was real. I stopped visiting him at the department stores and one day my mum said that we were going Christmas shopping to buy gifts for dad and my brother. So, by the time I was 8 or 9 I no longer believed in Santa Clause.

---

Roselyn with Santa Clause

**Time for you to do some work:**

Think about some of the beliefs you held in the past, maybe when you were a youngster, that have now been relegated to just a bygone thought?

I used to think that being half Chinese and half Australian in Australia meant that I was a second-class citizen. This belief was validated by my mother who thought she was protecting me by reminding me every morning that I was a "half caste" and other kids will look down on me, so work hard, behave and don't rock the boat.

The belief was further validated by the general community feeling in the 50's in Australia. It was not too long after World War II, so anyone who even looked slightly Asian was more often than not considered to be part of the cause of that tragedy.

In the early 70's I can remember my fiancé telling me that he had not yet told his grandmother that I was half Chinese because she had lost her husband in the war, and he didn't want her to think that he was a traitor to his grandfather's memory.

This belief led me to never seek the number one spot but carefully orchestrate it so that I always came second.

All through my teens and early adult life I would push the envelope just so far, just get a taste of what it was like to break out of the norm, and then just as it looked like I was going to make a substantial break through, I would somehow set myself up to pull back.

Over the years my environment changed and my inquisitive nature helped me to explore humanity and ask many questions. The net result is that at some point in time my belief that I was a second-class person faded into history and I started to go for the checkered flag.

*For many years I believed that only first-class citizens were allowed to do wonderful and amazing things is this world, and I was second class. .... Roselyn Poon*

**Basic reasons why your beliefs change:**

- Outside influences – your environment provides you with new information and experiences.
- An authority figure or mentor influences your thinking

- No longer relevant to you – some of your beliefs may be tied to a particular time in your life.
- No longer substantiated – you learn about new discoveries that negate earlier findings.
- A higher belief is created that negates lesser beliefs – you evolve personally and change your belief hierarchy.

---

The key to living a wonderful life is to be on the look-out and review your beliefs from time to time. Unfortunately, most humans set and forget everything... Roselyn

---

There is a sad story about an elephant which aptly demonstrates the power and durability of beliefs. The author is unknown but the moral of the story will stay with you.

---

Story: *As my friend was passing the elephants, he suddenly stopped, confused by the fact that these huge creatures were being held by only a small rope tied to their front leg. No chains, no cages. It was obvious that the elephants could, at any time, break away from the ropes they were tied to but for some reason, they did not. My friend saw a trainer nearby and asked why these beautiful, magnificent animals just stood there and made no attempt to get away.*

*"Well," he said, "when they are very young and much smaller, we use the same size of rope to tie them and, at that age, it's enough to hold them. As they grow up, they are conditioned to believe they cannot break away. They believe the rope can still hold them, so they never try to break free."*

*My friend was amazed. These animals could at any time break free from their bonds but because they believed they couldn't, they were stuck right where they were.*

---

Even elephants can be controlled by their beliefs.

## To Believe or Not to Believe, is the Question

Beliefs have the following characteristics:

- Beliefs can be challenged.
- Not all beliefs can be proven scientifically.
- Beliefs can be de-validated.
- Beliefs can be replaced.
- Beliefs can be changed.
- Beliefs can evolve.
- Beliefs can be set in stone.

The most important characteristic is the power your beliefs have over your life. I have spent a fair amount of time introducing you to the power and I strongly recommend checking out the topic further via Google and Amazon.

Belief is a fascinating topic on its own however in chapter 9 we are going to focus on your beliefs regarding time and aging so that you can reset your inner-clock and reclaim valuable years on our time line.

---

*In the words of John Greenleaf Whittier, the saddest words ever are "It might have been," or "I should have tired." The next saddest phrase is "I am too old to change." Don't let this be your epitaph.*

---

# Chapter 6

## Your State of Mind and Being

The final topic we need to cover before we can cure you of the Premature Aging Virus is your state. By this I mean your general well-being. What you think and feel about your life and yourself. This includes your feelings about various aspects of your life, for example:

- Self-esteem.
- Physical well-being.
- Economic well-being.
- Social well-being.
- Development and activity.
- Emotional well-being.
- Psychological well-being.
- Day to day life satisfaction.
- Engaging activities and work.

Personally, I am an optimist who is happy with my lot in life and excited about spreading the word on living younger longer. People don't need to know me very well to see that I am energized about life and happy. Apparently, my aura gives me away every time.

Personal story: Ever since I was a little girl our family doctor would declare how robust I was. Yes, he actually used the word robust. Thanks to him, I grew up very proud of being so healthy and I would tell people that my doctor says that I am built for the long haul. Even to this day I see myself as a very strong person who never gets sick, and guess what, I don't. When everyone is talking about the current flu epidemic, I simply explain that I don't get sick. I believe this and I subconsciously reinforce it by the way I talk about myself. How you refer to yourself and talk about yourself is a great insight into what you believe about yourself.

## Components of State

Your state is comprised of your "state of mind" and your "state of being". The term "state of mind" refers to your thoughts, attitudes, and feelings. Your "state of being" refers to your physical body, posture, body language, breathing, muscle tension, movement, and even where your eyes are directed.

STATE: total of state of mind and being

STATE OF MIND: psychological state

STATE OF BEING: physical state

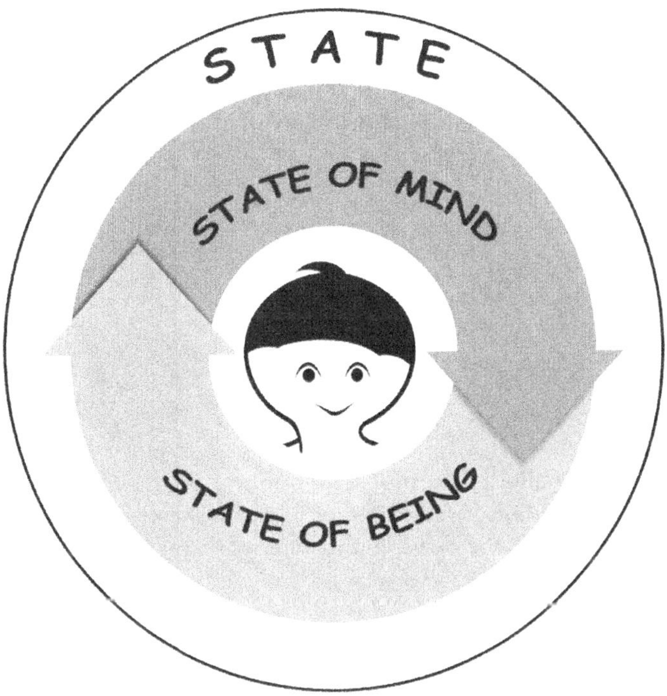

**Your state of mind**

Your state of mind is your emotional or mental state at a particular time. You wake up in a state of mind, you travel to work in a state of mind, you drink coffee in a state of mind and you even go to sleep in a state of mind.

Your state of mind colors your experience of life, and heavily influences your point of view, your decisions and your actions.

Example:

> If you see yourself as too old to learn how to text, you won't try to understand it, and when someone texts you, more than likely you will get frustrated and blame your old age for not being able to keep up with technology rather than your earlier decision to not bother learning about texting.
>
> The truth of the matter is that everyone has to learn how to use the latest technological tools, and even a teenager had to learn how to text. Learning is the determining factor in your ability to text, not your age.

> When we begin to diminish in our own eyes, the aging process hastens because it has to keep up with our fading view of ourselves. ....
>
> Vijay P. Sharma, Ph. D Clinical Psychologist

Your state of mind is affected by your state of being, your surroundings, things you read, see or hear, the time of day, time of year, sunshine, money, television, your friends, work colleagues, the news, music, information, experience, your beliefs, a touch; the list goes on forever.

Think about how your state of mind changes when you bump into an old friend, or get back to your car after a very successful meeting to find that you have a parking ticket. Think of a grandparent's probable state of mind when they see their first grandchild, or a deaf person when they can hear for the first time.

> Your state of mind is with you 24/7, however it is always changing.

My state of mind changes instantly when I hear a Porsche race car going through its paces. Think back to the times when your state of mind has changed due to an external influence?

What about those pesky weight scales that lurk in your bathroom waiting to mess with your head? How many times have you been feeling great and jumped on the scales to find that you have put on a couple of pounds? What did that do to your state of mind?

We all react differently to life because the building blocks of our state of mind are our beliefs which differ from one another. We may have the same basic core beliefs as other people, however the intensity and priority on our personal belief hierarchy may differ from one another.

**Example:** Your state of mind after successfully selling your property for a $50,000 profit is probably elation, whereas someone else may see it as a miserable outcome and feel disappointed. You see the $50,000 as a fantastic triumph and a great boost to your financial stability, whereas the other person may see it as a disaster and a complete waste of their time. You see it as a success and feel successful, whereas the other person sees it as a failure and may even feel like a failure.

During a professional Porsche car race at Calder Raceway in Melbourne, Australia, I drove my tail off keeping a seasoned driver from passing me. I was walking on air at the end of the race and anyone could be forgiven for thinking I had won. One of the greatest compliments I have ever received was from the driver I had blocked during that race. He declared to everyone that I had the widest Porsche he had ever raced behind, and commended my blocking skills.

Prior to the race I was feeling comfortable and quietly confident that I would bring the car home in one piece, however after the race I was jubilant and felt like I could conquer anything. Compare my reaction to the race winner who believed he was the fastest driver in the series and expected to win. It was no big surprise when he won, just another day at the track.

BTW: A couple of races later he came third and that had an impact on his state of mind.

Let's look at the two fundamental states of mind in more detail:

- Core state of mind – this is your basic personality, e.g. you are a glass half full or half empty person, or you are an optimist or pessimist. These are your core characteristics that filter and influence your experience of the world around you. Your core state of mind is shaped by your beliefs and responses to your environment, e.g. if your family members live into their 90's, you will grow up believing that you too will be kicking around into your 90's. Your belief dictates your core state of mind and subsequently your feelings and actions; because you believe you will live to a great age you will maintain your enthusiasm for life over the years and that will result in living to become a great age. It is a wonderful positive self-fulfilling cycle.

- Temporary state of mind – this is a transient state and can change constantly throughout the day, i.e. you feel miserable because you have the flu and because you feel miserable you feel useless, and because you feel useless you decide to decline the invite to join your friends on a week-end away. Two days later you are on top of the world because you are over the flu and wondering why you decided not to join your friends. Another example of our transient states of mind is feeling happy because you just watched an uplifting movie, and on the way home someone cuts you off in the traffic causing you to brake harshly. Instantly you go from happy to agitated and annoyed with the world.

> Transient states come and go throughout the day but your core state of mind is with you 24/7.

**Your state of being**

Your state of being is your physiological condition. How you are physically.

Example:

- Agile and limber
- Muscle sore
- Tense
- Headache
- Twisted ankle
- Healthy
- Terminally ill.

The important aspect of your state of being is that it affects your state of mind resulting in an overall state change. Even a small positive change in your physiology will cause amazing positive shifts in your state within seconds.

Example: You are feeling miserable because your eye is irritated and weeping. Suddenly, the irritation leaves your eye, the weeping stops and you are feeling relieved and happy.

**The relationship between your physical state of being and psychological state of mind**

Your psychology and physiology are intertwined. Your psychology has an effect on your physiology and vice versa.

Think back to the last time you had the flu or a very bad head cold. Your eyes were bloodshot, your nose was red and running, your head was foggy and your body felt like you had been hit by a Mack truck. Your usual upbeat enthusiasm for the day ahead was replaced with misery and self-pity, both of which are quite acceptable when one has the flu. Your poor physical state of being caused your usual enthusiastic state of mind to take a nose dive into the doldrums.

On the flip side, your state of mind affects your physiology. In my natural state, I start feeling sleepy around 9:45pm, and by 10:30pm I am on my way to bed. However, when I am up against a dead-line I can stay alert into the early hours of the morning without feeling the slightest bit tired.

Remember the times when your work demands caused you to put in a monumental effort and bypass your normal physiological states? Like myself, you probably have too many incidents to count.

Think back to those stories about amazing physical feats performed by mere mortals in times of extreme danger or stress? Mothers lifting cars to save trapped children, and prisoners of war surviving unimaginable torment are great examples of mind over matter.

Never underestimate the power of your state of mind.

Your state of mind and state of being work together, and depending on what is going on in your head and your world, one will win over the other or at least have an impact.

I wish it were possible for us to think away a terminal illness but at this point in time it is not generally accepted as feasible, however there are many documented cases of people who have been able to use their mind to cure themselves of major illnesses. However, right now, we are not looking into how we can use our mind to cure terminal illnesses, but rather how we can kick old age to the curb.

Personally, I believe that my state of mind is superior to my state of being, however they are forever joined, and as such one always follows the other.

Have you ever tried to stay angry with someone when all you wanted to do was laugh at them or smile? It's pretty difficult to feel angry or sad when your body is practicing happiness by smiling.

You don't have to feel terrific to smile. You can smile first and as a consequence of the relationship between smiling and feeling happy your state of mind will change to correlate with your smile – your state of being.

Through repetition your mind and body have forever linked together the physical act of smiling and the feeling of happiness. The relationship is such that a smile automatically triggers a response from your state of mind.

I felt an incredible sense of freedom when I became consciously aware that what I was thinking affected what I experiencing.

My experience of my world was pretty much up to me.

**Time for you to do some work:**

Let's try a simple test right now. Stop what you are doing and smile. Get into the smile. Can you sense a slight shift in your state? What is going through your mind? Have thoughts of times in the past that made you smile started popping into your mind, does the weight on your shoulders feel a bit lighter, do you feel more able, happier, less stressed?

It's amazing isn't it?

The simple physical act of smiling or laughing out loud can trigger a change in your state of mind.

If you aren't feeling it, keep practicing – what have you got to lose?

There is a never-ending interactive relationship between your beliefs, state of mind, state of being, environment and your response or experience of your environment.

Your beliefs affect your state of mind which covers feelings, thoughts, experiences, and your physical state of being. In turn, your state of being can affect your state of mind, beliefs, experiences and responses.

Your environment which includes people, places, media, the weather, activities, in fact your entire physical world affects every aspect of your life experiences. It affects your beliefs, state of mind, state of being and your experience of the world around you.

> Your state of mind and state of being are so interdependent that neither state can make a change without causing a shift in the other.

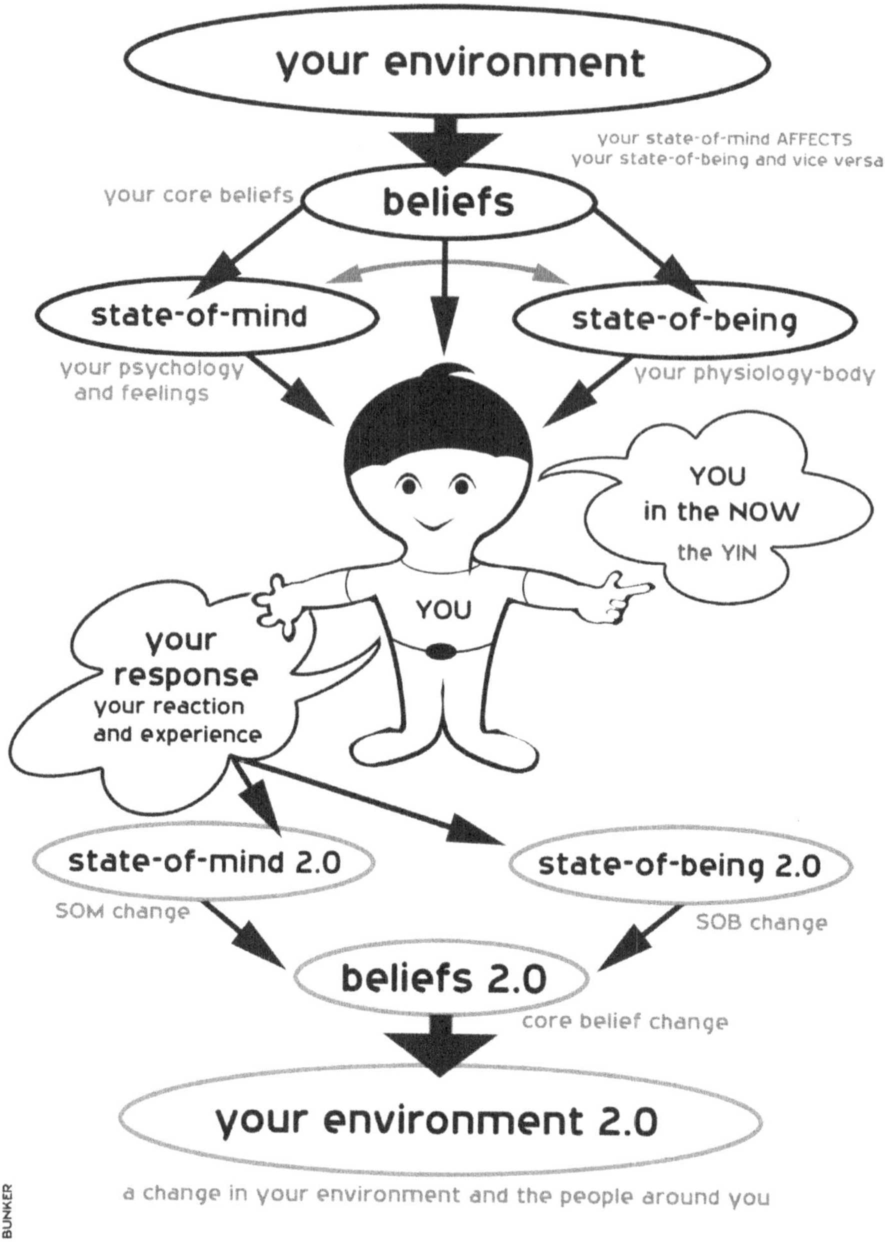


state - belief - environment - cycle

The diagram opposite demonstrates the iterative process you regularly go through without being over consciously aware of it.

Sometimes a state is updated or changed slightly but not every state and not every time.

Depending on what is going on in your world most state shifts are minor and temporary, however on occasion they will be more impactful.

**Example:** You are in a wonderful state of mind, the sun is shining, you are enjoying your walk in the park and then all of a sudden you slip on the wet grass. Instantly your state of being changes because you now have a sprained ankle. Your state of mind changes from happy and relaxed to stressed and anxious.

These are temporary state changes however if it turns out you have seriously damaged your ankle and need therapy for the next 12 months you may reconsider your belief that walking in the park is good for you.

**Example:** You love your home and neighbors, when one evening you hear a lot of loud music and cars zooming up and down your street. You realize that some of your more distant neighbors have moved out and been replaced with a different group of people. You stay put but over the coming year a few more of your neighbors relocate, and you realize that you no longer relate to your neighborhood and that you are quite depressed about life. This is an example of how progressive change can catch us unaware until we experience a serious shift in our state. Obviously, something has to change, either your environment, your beliefs, your state of mind, or your state of being. Let's be realistic, in that you are not going to be able to change your neighbors – you can only change what is in your control – you.

Check out what breathing with intention can do to your state of mind and overall state.

**Time to do some work:**

Stand up, stretch to the sky and breathe deep. Even if you can't stand or stretch, I know you can breathe so concentrate on that aspect.

Push that air down to your stomach and fill your entire lungs, not just the top half. Try to look like the Michelin Man or for those of you who are not into motor sport, imagine the Pillsbury Dough Boy.

Blow your cheeks out and imagine the oxygen straightening out all those little knots inside, push your tummy out further than ever before.

Then just before you are about to expire, blow all of that air out like you are trying to blow out the candles on your 100th birthday cake in a single breath.

You only need to do this a couple of times to make a positive shift in your physiological state and hence your state of mind and overall state.

I suggest you do this no more than 3 times in a row to avoid the possibility of hyperventilating with too much of a good thing, namely oxygen.

When you are standing tall, breathing deep and your eyes are looking straight ahead, it is pretty hard to feel small and down trodden. I just realized one of the reasons why I never felt depressed or beaten when racing, is that it is impossible to hunch over and look down when you are strapped into a molded racing seat by a five-point harness. You, the seat and the racecar are all one unit, just like your state of mind and state of being, forever linked to create your state.

The reason why you need to understand the relationships between environment, beliefs and your states is so that you can more easily see the elements that need your attention if you are to reclaim some lost years and slow down your aging.

**The flow on effect of your state**

Your state can affect someone else's state, and vice versa. We are living breathing entities and our energy responds to energy around us.

Have you ever started crying when someone around you is crying or better still started chuckling just because the people around you are laughing? After a minute or two it doesn't seem to matter that you have no idea why all of you are laughing.

> Personal story: I remember using this concept of flow on state of mind when I was the CEO of an information technology company. In spite of how I felt while driving to work, I would put a warm smile on my face and an enthusiastic spring in my step before I stepped into the office. It worked every time. Regardless of the problems the technical people had been experiencing before I arrived, they immediately felt more on top of things the moment they saw a warm confident person waiting to hear their concerns.

A fantastic side benefit of smiling and elevating your state of happiness is the flow on affect you will have on the people you come in contact with. Smiling can be contagious.

Feelings are contagious.

> There is an old saying that "misery attracts misery". I believe that the truth of the matter is that "misery creates misery". Roselyn

**Your state influences your success and failure**

It is amazing what we can do when we set our minds to it, or in other words, activate the right state of mind for the task at hand.

As I mentioned earlier, your state changes constantly throughout the day and night. The only thing we can be sure of is that your state is with you 24/7, but which exact state is in control at any point in time is the million-dollar question. This is why it is important for you to learn to manage your state's and use them for your greater good.

Before we can successfully do anything in life we need to be in the right state for that task. That means the most appropriate state of mind and the best corresponding physiological state of being... Roselyn

When I first started car-racing I thought all I needed was a winner's state of mind, and a racecar that could blow the door handles off the opposition. My enthusiasm and excitement took me through my first three-day race event without so much as a broken finger nail. I went to bed on the Sunday night feeling like I could walk on water, only to wake up the next morning feeling like I had been hit by a Mack truck. I had to roll out of bed and crawl to the phone to get help. I called Don, my race team manager, who just laughed, and I thought typical Aussie male reaction, sensitive to the bone, doesn't he understand, I am dying. Don is actually a very intelligent and intuitive guy and he explained that I had powered through the weekend event on pure mental energy, aka my state of mind, and now I was back on Mother Earth with what was left of my body, aka my state of being. It took a sports masseuse 3 hours to get me mobile again, and I learned a huge lesson. Not only did I need to nurture and coach my racing driver's state of mind but I needed to do the same to my state of being.

Thinking like a racing driver was not enough - I had to develop a racing driver's state of mind and physiology.

To be whatever it is that you want to be, you need the right state of mind and its corresponding physiological state of being. They work in harmony, like Yin and Yang, Tom and Jerry, Batman and Robin.

During my car racing career in Australia I met a young racing mechanic who was always busy and seemed permanently bent over, even when he walked, he reminded me of Groucho Marx minus the cigar. He was shy and pretty much ignored by everyone. While waiting for my racecar to be scrutineered before a race, we got chatting and my curiosity got the better of me so I asked him how tall he was. To my surprise he said 6'2", and I said, "You're pulling my leg". With that, he stepped back from the railing and stood up straight. Well, what a difference a few inches make. All of a sudden, he looked like a confident and knowledgeable young racing technician, instead of a dithering hunched over grease monkey. I was so shocked I had to tell him about the amazing difference in my impression of him once he stood up. We talked about it for another few minutes, and from that moment onwards he has walked tall. His confidence shone out and people could see his eyes and his great smile, and people responded to him differently. This caused his confidence and self-esteem to grow and within months he became one of the most sought-after Porsche race mechanics in Melbourne.

Now, I am not promising that you can become an international jet setting motor mechanic just by standing straighter, but I can promise you that with some conscious effort on your behalf into managing your state of mind and your state of being you will be rewarded many times over.

Quick recap:

- Your state is comprised of your state of mind and your state of being.
- Your state of mind and state of being work together.
- Your state is all powerful and with you 24/7.
- Your state changes throughout the day and night.
- Knowing which state, you are in and how to manage your states is a huge step towards increasing your success in life.

## Managing Your State

Car racing has taught me a great deal about the importance of managing my state. State management involves being aware of the state you are currently in, and knowing what state you need to be in to achieve your desired outcome.

*In fact, racing is a constant state awareness and management game with the added complication of the race car's physiology and temperament. It is the same with everyday driving. If your car is missing a beat, doesn't this have an effect on your feeling of security driving it and consequently, how you drive it?*

Several times prior to a race, I would close my eyes and imagine the entire race, the count down to the green light, turn one, every corner, every gear change, every squeal of my tires, the checkered flag and the look of elation and pride on my team members after a great race. I would go over and over right up until we were called onto the track.

> Practicing in my mind not only dialed in the right state of mind for the race, but it also triggered the right physiological state of being.

My body is comprised of more slow twitch muscles than fast twitch which means that I am better suited to long distance endurance events rather than sprinting. It takes a while for my body to get moving, however once moving it can go forever. Porsche racing is all about sprinting and luckily my personal fitness trainer understood this. He taught me how to get my body moving before the race. I drank hot spicy Indian tea and practiced breathing sharp and fast. My mind and body were already racing by the time I was at the start line.

It is also important to understand the many states you experience throughout your day, week, month, year. Being aware of your state is the first step to managing the states you want to be in, rather than just accepting the states that pop up as a result of habit and things around you.

I have found that for very important states it is best to give them a name. This means that in one or two words I can invoke the required state.

Example: I call my racing driver state of mind the Gladiator. One word invokes an entire shift in my state of mind and associated physiological state of being.

When I am racing my Porsche, I become my version of a gladiator. I instantly feel strong and powerful. My jaw tightens and my breathing becomes deeper. My mind is laser focused on getting through the pack.

When you meet me, you will fully appreciate how powerful the shift in my state of being really is. During my last medical my doctor tried to tell me I was only 5'3" tall and weighed 132lbs soaking wet, but she should see me when I am the Gladiator. I am 6' tall and all muscle.

I have developed a whole bunch of state's that I invoke when required, e.g.

- Athlete – I use this state when I am working out at the gym. I automatically train with intention. I constantly visualize myself looking great.

- Problem Solver – I become a great listener and empathize with the people I am listening to. I genuinely want to know what they have to say.

There are many more, for example, the dancer, entertainer, speaker, friend, older sister, daughter, educator, leader, protector and sleep head. These are temporary state's each with its own feelings and physiological state.

The magic is in knowing that you can manage your states or at least have some conscious input into which state of mind is happening, and what your body is doing from time to time.

My practice of going through the race in my mind was so vivid. It included the sound of the howling of the Porsche engines and the vision of the fleet of race bred machinery covered in their war paint. My physiology transformed from instantly from anxious to gladiator. My mind truly believed I was racing. My shoulders would square off, my spine would straighten, my chest would expand and my breathing would slow down and feel strong and powerful. It didn't start out like this. The buildup of my Gladiator state took time and practice.

> I didn't have much to go on when I started developing my Gladiator state. I used my imagination.

I started by asking questions of other race drivers and asking myself what I thought it would feel like, how would I look, how would my team members look and feel after a great performance.

> I just kept asking questions of myself and the people I met in the motor racing game. Of course, the best answers came when I started having a go and getting out on the track.

I started from my imagination which was at least a start and I continued to improve on my Gladiator state every chance I got. These days even listening to a soundtrack of a Porsche screaming off down the straightaway invokes my Gladiator state.

> Awareness is the first step towards change.

"You are a long time dead" is a famous saying, however the way society has us currently thinking, a more relevant saying today is "You are a long time being old".

Get off that train speeding to the human scrap heap and take control. Create a new motto for yourself like "I am forever young.", "She who drives makes the decisions" and one of my favorite racing mottos is "She who signs the checks, gets to play."

## Recap of State of Mind and State of Being

- Your state is the sum total of your state of mind and being.
- Your state of mind is with you 24/7.
- Your state of mind changes throughout the day.
- Your state of mind and physiological state of being are linked and have a direct effect on each other.
- Your physiology can be altered by your state of mind.
- Your state of mind can be affected by your physiology.
- Your state of mind can also be affected by everything and everyone around you.
- You have multiple states of mind thus states, depending on circumstances.
- Each one of your states of mind is the result of your beliefs in context with your circumstance.

# Chapter 7

## Review and Outline on How to Cure Your Premature Aging Virus

The principal function of this book is to make you aware of three things:

- you have the Premature Aging Virus which is causing you to age faster than necessary
- you can cure yourself of the Premature Aging Virus
- you can reclaim years and reset your inner clock now.

### CHAPTER 1: THE PREMATURE AGING VIRUS

- you are born with the PAV pre-loaded into your sub-conscious
- the PAV affects every decision you make
- you are aging in accordance with your environment
- time is a man-made construct to enable scheduling
- you age because your biology is deteriorating not because of time
- age is like a page number in a book, it has no relevance to the story line

### CHAPTER 2: HOW YOU CONTRACTED THE PREMATURE AGING VIRUS

- starting out life as a passenger on the Old Age Express
- generic time line ends around station 80
- your environment from birth, the media, people you associate with, financial institutions, ageism, and technology all feed the PAV which keeps aging you in accordance with their accepted norms

**CHAPTER 3: THE PAIN OF OLD AGE**

- there are 4 ways to gauge your age: biological, social, chronological and the most important psychological.
- psychological age is the only way to age, if you have to age at all
- old age has nothing to offer except for issues around health, finances, government forms, alienation, loss of independence and stress just to name a few
- old age isn't a battle, it is a massacre
- you worked out where you are in your life journey and what is going to be your next station on the Old Age train line

**CHAPTER 4: THE AMAZING ALTERNATIVE TO OLD AGE**

- the discovery that there is an alternative to growing old at your current rate
- there is no downside to clawing back 10 – 20 years of your time line
- resetting your inner clock and proceeding forward with the benefit of hind sight
- time to build your nest egg for the time when you decide to take it easy
- key benefit to you is the time to do whatever it is you want to do without the stress of worrying about running out of time

**CHAPTER 5: THE POWER OF BELIEFS**

- your beliefs control how you interpret and respond to your experience of life
- your beliefs run on automatic in your sub-conscious
- most of the time a belief is created and never revisited even if conditions change
- your beliefs are created and reinforced by your environment
- beliefs can change if you are aware of them
- thoughts are transient and may become beliefs if they are frequent and have feelings attached to them
- managing your beliefs is the prime component to curing you of the Premature Aging Virus

**CHAPTER 6: YOUR STATE OF MIND & BEING**

- your state is comprised of your state of mind and your state of being

- state of mind is your psychological state, what you feel and believe
- state of being is your physical state, biology
- state of being and state of mind are forever intertwined and affect each other
- your core state is the most powerful determinant of your life experience
- your state of mind is a by-product of your beliefs however it is affected by varying degrees by your state of being
- you can create states for specific functions
- you can manage your states and invoke the appropriate state for the job at hand
- it is critical to have the right state active to increase your chance of success

## You Now Know

- most people age in accordance with what their environment believes is normal
- it is possible to defer old age for a period of time, reset your inner clock and reclaim the last 10 – 20 years
- you know of at least one person who has reset their inner clock and reclaimed 20 years – me
- there is no upside to getting older, and no downside to working on reclaiming the last 10 years
- you know that you can jump off the Old Age Express anytime and take control of your aging
- now let's look at how you reclaim those years. The following chapters will take you through the process of resetting your inner clock

## Moving Forward

### CHAPTER 8: STARTING WITH THE RIGHT STATE OF MIND

- activating the best state of mind for the job at hand of resetting your inner clock and getting those valuable years
- there is no point in trying to take control of your aging if you don't believe it is possible – you have to believe to get the best start possible – worst case scenario is to proceed on blind faith because you have nothing to lose and a great deal to gain

**CHAPTER 9: OLD AGE BELIEFS AND YOU**

- what's happening in the world of biology and science
- what do you believe?
- what is really relevant these days

**CHAPTER 10: MOVING FROM OLD TO BOLD**

- NLP
- Kaizen
- Vision Boards
- Goal Setting
- Neuroplasticity

*Bronnie Ware worked with the dying for many years and penned a book titled "The Top Five Regrets of the Dying". Bronnie found that the most common regrets which surfaced time and time again are:*

*Regret 1 - I wish I'd had the courage to live a life true to myself, not the life others expected of me.*

*Regret 2 - I wish I didn't work so hard.*

*Regret 3 - I wish I had the courage to express my feelings.*

*Regret 4 - I wish I had stayed in touch with my friends.*

*Regret 5 - I wish I had let myself be happier.*

# Chapter 8

# Starting with the Right State of Mind

Your quality of life is dependent on your core state of mind.

......... Roselyn

## Step One is to Get into the Right State of Mind to Reset Your Inner Clock

In Chapter 5 we talked about the belief hierarchy, and the most influential belief is that which pertains to your feelings of self-esteem. This covers your beliefs on your self-worth and what you believe you are capable of achieving.

This chapter is an exercise in personal discovery.

**Are you reluctant to live younger longer?**

Do you have compelling reasons which cause you to want to spend valuable years in old age?

- Are you tired of life?
- Does living seem like hard work?
- Do you look into the future and see more lonely long days?
- Do you see benefits in old age?
- Do you like people caring for you?
- Do you like people worrying about you?
- Do you like controlling people around you?
- Do you like the attention being old brings you?

I am sure we have all had times when life just seemed too hard and not worth the effort, however in most cases these thoughts are fleeting. However, if they have taken up permanent residence in your mind, you need to seriously look at the benefits of evicting them.

Consider the possibility that reframing your thinking about your age and your timeline may give you a new fresh outlook on your life. Maybe with a little bit of work your life might not seem so tiresome. Personally, I was tired and depressed before I realized I could reset my inner clock to a more youthful and helpful phase. The realization alone gave me hope and helped to change my state of mind.

The point is that your experience of life and your state of mind are integrated, and as a consequence they affect each other. You know you are going to pass from this life sometime, no matter how diligent you are with reframing your beliefs and state of mind, I am simply asking you to consider giving this whole reframing state of mind thing a go. What have you got to lose?

---

There is no failure and there could even be some success. Only you can decide, because it is your life.

---

Firstly, you need to become familiar with the characteristics of your current state of mind. You need to be able to recognize it as quickly as you recognize your partner or your neighbor. The best way to do this is to ask yourself lots of questions and imagine that you are sending your answers to someone living on the other side of the world. If you are a person who can easily visualize things then describe your answers in terms of what you can see, include size, movement, brightness, contrast and color. If you are more into sounds, describe what you can hear, include volume, tone, tempo, clarity, distance, voices and music. Finally, if you are more into feelings, try describing your answers in terms of how it feels, including sensations, temperature, shape and what part of your body you are experiencing these feelings.

We describe ourselves based on our beliefs, e.g. I am a klutz, I never get the girl, I always leave things to the last minute, I always come last. It is your identity. This is how you identify yourself. You need to become conscious of your unconscious self talk. You could be brain washing yourself into the grave.

**Let's look at your core state**

**Time for you to do some work:**

Some good questions to ask yourself to start the ball rolling are:

How do you feel most of the time? Are you down, sad, energized, optimistic, sunny, grumpy, hopeful, strong, conflicted or ho hum?

Does life feel heavy or uplifting?

Are you mainly optimistic or pessimistic about life?

What are you hearing right now? Is there so much noise going on in your head that you can't hear yourself think, or is tranquil, quiet, empty or distant?

**Now let's look at your feelings about aging and your life ahead**

**Time for you to do some work:**

In a few words how would you describe yourself and your feelings about your life thus far?

What words come to mind first?

How do you describe yourself when speaking to others?

How do you refer to yourself in your own mind?

Do you find that you often say; 'I am too old for that' or 'It's never too late to give it a go'?

Who or what type of people do you identify with?

What type of people do you easily relate to?

Does your future look like more of the same or lots of colorful boxes waiting to be opened?

How do you feel about your future? Excited, no comment, tired?

Does time feel like it is zooming ahead way too fast?

How far into the future can you see, to the end of your nose, lunch time, your next holidays or as far as 5, 10, 15 years?

Do you believe age is just a number and has no bearing on your life, or do you cringe at every birthday and subconsciously adjust your state of mind to match the text book description of someone at that age?

Do you find that you often say; 'I am too old for that' or 'It's never too late to give it a go'?

List the things you feel you can't do because of your age.

List things you would like to do but you feel are inappropriate due to your age or you believe it is too late.

List things that you feel are appropriate for your age.

How many productive years and life years do you genuinely believe you have remaining?

Define what productive years means to you.

Why did you come up with these figures?

List why you feel you have "x" number of productive years left.

Do you want to end up dependent upon family members and welfare?

Do you want to wake up with a renewed energy for life?

Do you want to reset your inner clock and get back years?

If you want to reset your inner clock and get back years, write down why it is so important to you and include the alternative. This gives you a carrot and the stick.

Once you have described your core state of mind and answered all of the questions about your feelings towards aging and your future, I would like you to combine the answers and give it a name, e.g. Old State, Older State, or Old Me. Referencing a name is a lot easier than detailing all the components every time you want to make a personal comparison or change.

Now, I want you to simply accept your current core state of mind. Don't judge it and don't try to change it just yet. Slosh around in it. See if you can see for yourself how it has affected your responses to the world around you, thus far. Do you think you might have had the same responses if you were ten or twenty years younger?

You are reading this book because something is starting to make you feel uncomfortable in your seat on the Old Age Express.

Feeling uncomfortable is the first step to introspection and evolution.

> The alternative to being a passenger on the Old Age Express is to accept that you can control your aging, reclaim some lost years and map out your own journey travelling at your own speed.

It is your core state of mind that determines if your everyday life is wonderful, difficult, sad, exciting or just plain dull.

All of your little habits and pet phrases give you clues as to your core state of mind which dictates your core state.

If you have trouble working out what your core state of mind is, try asking a good friend to describe you in their words, with the proviso that you will still be good friends afterwards.

Before you can start the process of pushing old age as far into the future as possible, you need to understand what your state of mind is regarding old age and yourself. You need to understand your core beliefs about aging, old age, and where you feel you are in your timeline.

Regardless of what your current state of mind is regarding old age and you, it can always use a bit of a lift, and knowing how you feel about it will help you to play a more active role in your future aging.

## Are You Scared of Trying to Reset Your Inner Clock for Fear of Failure?

Are you more concerned with possible failure than possible success?

Tony Robbins says that we are more concerned with pain than pleasure. This is an interesting thought in that if you truly believe this, then maybe we need to take a look at how you define the word fail.

**Time for you to do some work:**

How do you define failure?

Write down all the words, colors and feelings that the word "failure" conjures up in your world.

When would you say you have 'failed' in the past?

To be fair we should look at your understanding of the word success.

**Time for you to do some work:**

How do you define success?

List the words, colors and feelings that come to mind when you think about success, e.g. personally, success is when I continue to make advances every week. It is the color yellow and a feeling of strength.

When would you say that you have experienced success?

I have often heard people say that you haven't failed until you give up. We Aussies believe that in between failure and success is having a go. Having a go is a common Aussie term. It means we are not sure of the outcome but having a go is better than sitting on our hands. Having a go only stops when we reach the success goal or give in to failure.

> Have a go!

How often have you read where scientists have spent years experimenting to produce a certain drug, and in doing so have invented many other wonderful things along the way. There is something to be said for the journey. Do you think that you might be able to think of living younger longer as a journey rather than a goal?

> If there is no deadline so to speak, then maybe there is no real failure point.

The person who has the all-time record at failing is Edison. He ultimately stopped failing at inventing the electric light bulb after having a go 1,000 times. He is reported as saying that, "Our greatest weakness lies in giving up. The most certain way to succeed is always to try just one more time."

Are you willing to put in the work?

It's your choice.

The alternative to a slow drawn out old age is to take control of your aging process now and focus on a brighter younger future.

## Do You Think It Might Be Too Late to Start Thinking Younger?

> Believing that it is too late to reframe your thinking is probably one of the nastiest limiting beliefs there is.

Do you believe that you don't have the time to learn how to change your mind set on aging and getting old? This is a serious limiting belief. I won't lie to you, there will be some work however:

> You are fighting for your life so what bigger battle is there worthy of your focus and intention?

A friend once said to me that aiming for the moon was a worthy goal even if you know you will never get there because of the things you will see and learn while trying. Experiences that you would never have if you had not made the decision to reach for the moon.

If you don't think you have time to reframe your thinking on aging and get back 10 years, that is ok. The next five years are going to come and go regardless of what you do or don't do. Wouldn't it be wonderful if you learned something new, met a few interesting people, had a couple of new experiences and smiled a bit more? So, what if you don't completely reframe your thinking on aging and get back 20 years. Just by taking a few steps towards that goal you will create some new feelings and you may even get back a year or two. Doesn't this sound better than growing older every day with nothing to look forward to other than the end of the line?

> The end of the line is happening sooner or later no matter what you do or don't do, so why not have a go! ... Roselyn

Only you can answer the questions of how old you want to live to and what kind of journey you want to experience along the way. I can't answer that for you. What I can do is make you aware that you have a choice. You can run your own race, not someone else's. It's like learning how to be a racing driver or learning how to do anything; you have to want it and then you have to work at it!

**Feeling that are too old to learn new tricks?**

> Can't teach an old dog new tricks.

What a load of rubbish. You are never too old to learn. You may be too old to implement them, or you might not be as efficient as younger ones but you can certainly learn. Once you become an adult, I don't believe learning is age dependent. The speed and degree of skill depends on the individual not your age.

The example I use to demonstrate this is teaching people how to bang a nail into a piece of wood. It seems pretty simple. There's a piece of wood, a nail and a hammer. You could pull ten people off the street and out of the ten, probably one person is going to be able to hit that nail straight in. Six people will probably hurt their fingers or, damage themselves in some way. Two will more than likely lose or bend the nail and one will throw the hammer at you.

To reclaim 10 – 20 years of your time line back depends on how geared up, and motivated you are to learn the skills of reprogramming your beliefs and managing your state of mind. You are unique and the degree of success, effort and time depends on you alone. I don't subscribe to the famous saying: 'if I can do it, you can'. Not everyone can do it, however the important point is that you are aware that you have an alternative to spending a quarter of your life in old age, which means you can make an informed decision on giving it a go or not.

Just to add to that, you have years more of valuable experience than you had back in your 30's, 40's, and 50's, and you've just added 20 more psychological years to your life timeline; use it wisely. This is valuable stuff.

It's about taking control of your beliefs and thoughts that can release you from the artificial chains keeping you on the Old Age express. If you can get rid of those limitations, through your belief systems; just think of the things you can accomplish.

> Achieving worthy goals frequently involves adopting new routines that you may not currently find fun or desirable. But they are essential for your success.

LAS VEGAS REVIEW-JOURNAL®
reviewjournal.com
October 15, 2015

COBRA COUTURE

# Designer transitions skills learned from auto industry into fashion

## Graphic patterns used to enhance women's figures

**By Sandy Lopez**
View staff writer

Women's bodies and car designs may seem like two very different things, but fashion designer **Bunker Hill Bradley** knows that the appeal is all in the curves.

The automobile designer switched to women's fashion two years ago after his partner in life and business, **Roselyn Poon**, wanted to find a dress that could cover certain areas and enhance others.

He went to the drawing board.

"There's a hidden formula in each graphic pattern that enhances the female figure," Bradley said. "I use my artistic means to draw the eyes and attentions to certain areas of the body."

By using curves, colors and adding shading, he essentially uses the same technology he learned in the car industry to create his visual designs under the name Cobra Couture. The name came from the way the company's dresses slip onto a woman's body like a "second skin."

**Fashion designer Bunker Hill Bradley holds a Cobra Couture Miracle Dress inside the headquarters of Cobra Couture in North Las Vegas Sept. 28. Without the use of buttons, belts or zippers, Bradley creates original pieces to highlight the female body.** SANDY LOPEZ/VIEW

"Ladies who put on the Miracle Dress feel happy and feel like partying," Bradley said. "We take quite a different approach to fashion than most other people. For us, it's all about comfort."

The North Las Vegas couple said their clothing line is designed for women of any age and of any profession.

Without the use of buttons, belts or zippers, Bradley creates original pieces to highlight the female body. His dresses pop with bright orange and pink or aqua combinations.

After hearing one customer declare that the dress was a "miracle," the couple adopted the name Miracle Dress.

The dresses range from $180 to $275, depending on how much fabric is used.

In addition to their dresses, they have 30 styles of swing coats, which Poon describes as a European style, and they sell palazzo pants, which look like bell bottoms but are created with polyester-spandex.

Although Cobra Couture has only been a Las Vegas fashion name for roughly two years, it has received attention in the spotlight.

Bradley designed the 2013 costume of the wine angels of Charlie Palmer's Aureole restaurant at Mandalay Bay, and the company has done eight fashion shows around town.

From broadcast reporter to lawyers, Poon said locals are noticing their designs, but it hasn't come without its challenges.

"I wanted the colors to look as bright as they did on the computer," Bradley said. "It took me a while to find the right fabric, which is our little secret. It won't wrinkle, and you can take off a stain fairly easily."

Those interested in purchasing an item can set up an appointment with Poon, who will choose a well-fitting dress to start.

"When a customer comes in, I sort of have a look and ask them what they like about their body and what they don't like," Poon said. "Some people don't like their tummy, or they feel they have big hips. I will just pick out what I think is a good fit, and then I step out of the way. I've heard one woman say, 'My god, I lost 12 pounds.'"

For more information, call Poon at 949-241-3996 or visit cobraculture.com.

**FOR THE FULL STORY, VISIT VIEWNEWS.COM.**

*— To reach North View reporter Sandy Lopez, email slopez@viewnews.com or call 702-383-4686. Find her on Twitter: @JournalismSandy.*



Article: It is possible to re-invent yourself, like Bunker has here.

## Transient States

**How do you feel right now?**

How you feel can vary in intensity and importance. A state of joy at finding a car parking spot in a busy street is fleeting, and possibly important for that instance but the feeling is gone as soon as you get out of your car.

My self-esteem is fairly good however that doesn't stop me from feeling disappointed with myself when I sneak some of Bunker's sugary pastries. The point is that this feeling of disappointment is fleeting and has no bearing on my core state of self-confidence. However, if I were to constantly dwell on feeling that I was letting myself down, it would start to manifest itself in all manner of things and then it has an impact on my overall self-esteem.

The key is to become aware of some of your intense temporary states which allows you to consciously decide if they are undesirable and hence temporary, or maybe the beginning of something very worthwhile.

Examples of temporary states – each has its own level of importance and priority:

- Feeling hungry, tired or weary
- Feeling worried about something but not sure what
- Feeling like you have run out of time and it is too late to do some of the things you wanted to do a few years back
- Feeling a little defeated by life and sad that you have not explored your potential more
- Feeling excited about an upcoming vacation

**Time for you to do some work:**

Describe your everyday overall state which includes your physical state of being and your state of mind. Bear in mind you probably have one state for work days and a different state for your days off.

Let's call these your basic states, and I suggest giving them a name to easily differentiate between them.

Example: Work state and Weekend state.

During the day you will also experience a variety of state changes that will last for seconds to hours, for example your Work state might get a lift if you receive a great response to your project presentation. Your Weekend state may get a hit if your sports team loses. These shifts are temporary and fade over time.

---

Your beliefs have a major influence over your state of being. It is very difficult to feel like a winner when you believe that you are a looser.

---

## Creating Your Living Younger State of Mind

Just like I needed to learn how to live younger, you also need to learn how to live younger and to run our own race.

This starts with learning how to be a driver rather than a passenger. You need to remember or learn what it feels like to make your own life decisions and not simply go with the flow. Become aware of your surroundings and begin to review what is important to you. In the following chapters we will reveal to your conscious self some of your long-held beliefs regarding aging and where you are in your timeline, for the purpose of evaluating their relevance to your future.

You need to know what the future can be like when you are the driver. Sure enough, we will all get the black flag in the end, but we have considerable input into how we get there. Prior to my understanding of aging and taking control of my future, it looked like one long slow stream of miserable days filled with regret and sadness. These days I have exciting plans that stretch for decades.

Earlier in this chapter you gave your current everyday state a name, now you are going to ask yourself some questions that will help you get started on creating the state of mind you need to become the winning racing driver in the race of your life. This new state is going to become one of your top ten states so give it a great name. A name that instantly invokes all the wonderful pictures, sounds and feelings it represents.

Example: Super Me, Younger Me, The Driver.

This name is only needed until you evolve into the version of you who is genuinely younger, at which point in time your living younger state will simply be you.

Some of the generic characteristics of a living younger mind set are:

- a strong belief that I control my aging
- deep desire to get back years and go forward with a more enthusiasm
- happy in the knowing that I have a chance to do the things I thought I had run out of time to do
- ignore naysayers
- open minded and interested in latest aging medical research
- passionate about life
- I have a big enough why to live younger longer
- want to know more about living younger longer
- enthusiastic about resetting my inner clock
- starting now, don't want to wait one more minute.

When answering the following questions, I want you to stretch your imagination, and even if you have never experienced what you are describing just try to imagine what it would feel like if you could.

Make your answers as big and colorful as possible by adding sound, movement, smells and feelings. Include friends, family and people. Imagine that you are Spielberg or Disney. The sky is the limit. Take your time with these questions and thoroughly think through your answers.

*This is your chance to fantasize and be as creative as your heart's desire. The Thought Police are nowhere in sight.*

**Remember you have put your current state of mind on hold for the moment.**

Imagine you are 10 years younger than your chronological age, and answer the questions from the view point of this younger you. You are not going back in time and revisiting your past. You are closing your eyes and telling yourself that when you open your eyes you are ten years younger, and say the actual number, e.g. if you are chronologically 65 now, tell yourself you are 55 when you open your eyes. Nothing else has changed except your age.

These questions are designed to start you thinking and feeling as the younger you. The feeling and hearing parts are critical to creating a compelling state of mind.

**Time for you to do some work:**

Spend as much time as you need on answering these questions. The more detail you can muster up, the more vivid and real your picture will become and the bigger your rewards will be.

How do you feel now that you are 10 years younger – happy, curious, relaxed, positive, healthier, more awake, emotionally less stressed and feeling lighter, enthusiastic, strong? Personally, I felt a great sense of relief because I was no longer stressing over the clock.

How do you feel physically – healthy, agile, ready to try some outdoor hiking, considering taking up a walking program, or catching up with old friends?

What can you hear around you – voices, music, nature, are the sounds light and airy or dark and scary?

How do you feel when you think about your future? What does the future look like from this position? What color is the future – white, yellow, bright, pale, black and white or psychedelic?

How far into the future can you see, to the end of your nose, lunch time, your next holidays or as far as 5, 10, 15 years?
Can you see the end or does it stretch on forever like those summer days when you were a kid?

How does the world look now that you are 10 years younger?

Did you discover that you are a natural story teller or was it hard going? If you found it a bit tough the first time around, that's ok, just go back to the start and give it another go. In car racing we have a saying that nothing beats "bum in seat time", translated this means that nothing produces better race results than hours of physically driving your racecar on a race track. Keep building on your answers. Remember this is your future and you are the driver.

Your younger state of mind is going to develop over time and with practice as soon as you start using it. Update your vision of the future as the Younger You whenever possible, and even better record your answers. I find recording a lot easier than writing, and it is more usable. I can replay it when I am stuck in traffic or soaking in the tub. The best time to replay it is just as you are falling asleep, think of it as your own personal bedtime story.

The more you go over the questions and build bigger and brighter pictures or symphonies for those of us who are more audio than visual, the more compelling and real your Younger state of mind will become.

Remember, you are just starting out so your answers are based pretty much on your imagination, however try it on, see how it fits, wear it around for a while and then revisit it.

You are on a journey of discovery which by definition means you will experience and discover new teachings along the way which will color your view of the future. Your future will continue to expand every time you step into your Younger state of mind.

It was this exercise of going into the future that morphed me into an excited 32-year-old with a terrific future ahead of me, whereas a few seconds earlier I was about to throw myself off a bridge in despair.

This process works, and I should know because this is how I started this whole living younger longer mission, although at the time I didn't know it. However, bear in mind that we are unique and your experience will be different to mine and that is fine with the universe. Just make sure you have a go and step into the future that is being created by the Younger you.

> Remember nothing has changed except your state of mind which affects how you see the world around you and this changes everything from this point forward.
>
> It isn't much fun watching your favorite movie with no sound and in black and white - so be creative.

Time for you to do some work:

List at least 20 characteristics of YOUR younger state of mind.

## Habitually Check Your State

Creating a youthful energized state of mind is only part of the process of creating a long healthy life. The other side is to reduce your negative aging self talk and toxic states. The best way to start doing this is to ask yourself 3 or 4 times a day how you are feeling – set an alarm in your phone or clock if you have to. It is crucial that you become aware of your states during the day.

> You ask everyone you meet how they are today, so how about asking yourself.

To demonstrate how toxic negative self talk is, I want to tell you a story about a beautiful woman who is about to become 40 years of age. This lady I know is very worried about turning 40; she is constantly bemoaning the onset of her 40's, and is absolutely positive that 40 signifies that she is officially old. Her birthday is not for another nine months! Unfortunately, if she continues down this path with this state of mind, by her $40^{th}$ birthday she will have convinced her unconscious that she is old. She is sending her toxic message to her unconscious at least 100 times a day, 24/7. This is brain washing at its most deadly because it is relentless. Sadly, she is already showing signs of aging in her daily decision making.

> Check your state and make sure that it is working for you and not against you.

Get into the habit of checking what state you are in. It is very easy to slip into complacency. If you are feeling old, tired and out of date, consciously invoke your Younger Me state. Go for a walk around the block, call a friend, get out of the house, any of these simple actions will be enough to allow you to invoke your Younger Me state. The trick is to be aware of your state and take steps to invoke the state you want. If you don't keep watch on your state of mind you could be heading for a miserable unhealthy and unforgiving old age.

> You are with yourself 24/7 so keep tabs on your state of mind and your self talk. You don't want to brain wash your unconscious into thinking that you have one foot in the grave and the other on a banana peel.

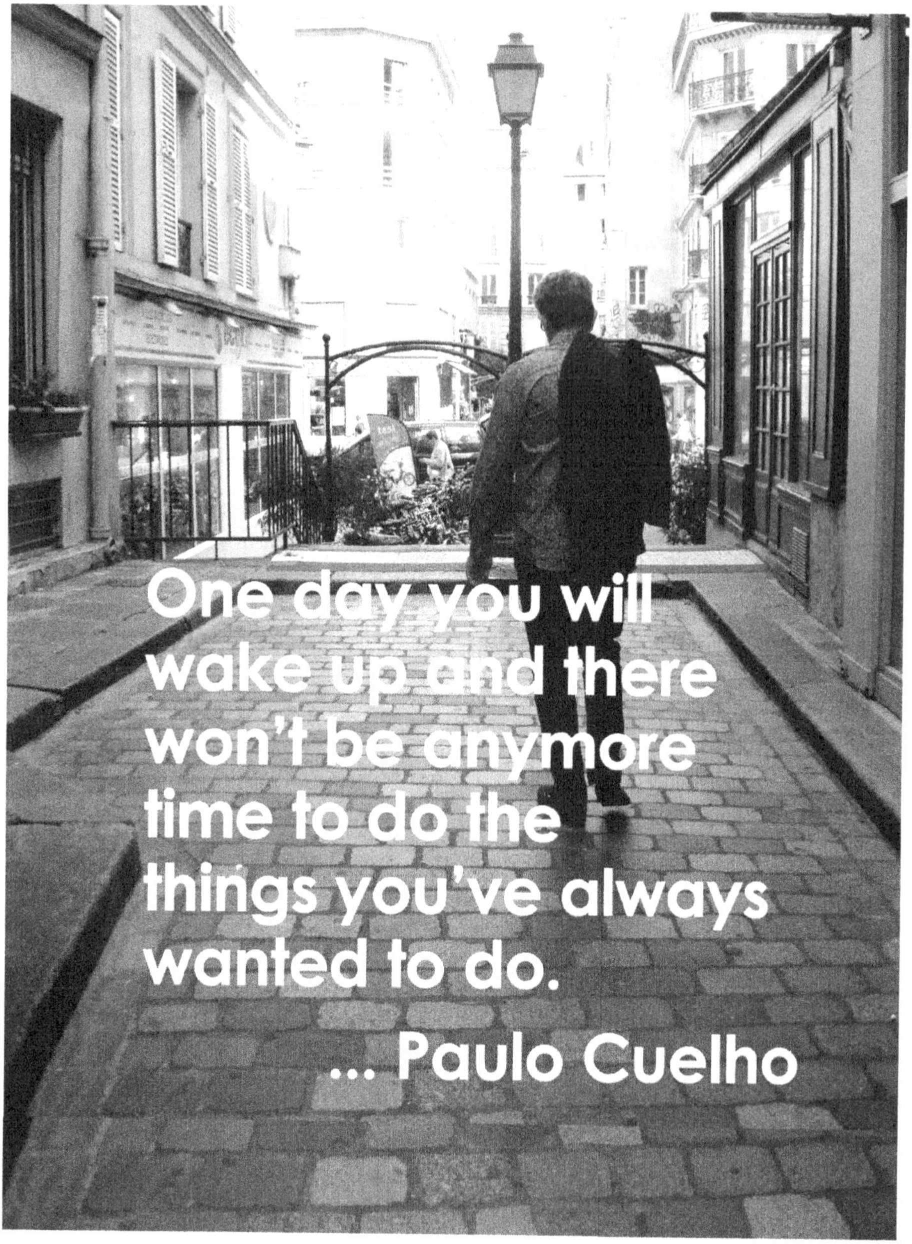
One day you will wake up and there won't be anymore time to do the things you've always wanted to do.
... Paulo Cuelho

# Chapter 9

## Old Age Beliefs & You

Studies have shown that negative self-perception reduces lifespan by seven and one-half years! ....... Becca Levy, Social and Behavioral Science Department, Yale School of Public Health, New Haven, Connecticut, United States of America.

Earlier we talked about how beliefs are created and their power over your life. Now we need to drill down and look at specific premature aging issues that keep the Premature Aging Virus flourishing.

Environmental and cultural beliefs are the main contributing causes of the PAV:

- growing old is natural
- retirement
- too late to start and/or change
- brainwashing by your environment and the media
- the future belongs to the young
- ageism
- technology
- environmental brainwashing

Unhealthy beliefs about yourself constantly keep the PAV alive and can even dissuade you from having a go at resetting your inner clock. Example:

- your self-worth - are you worth the effort to reframe your thinking about aging
- your ability – beliefs you have about your ability to reset your inner clock
- too ill to change now
- old equals brain dead
- your why - do you have big enough benefits for resetting your inner-clock

## Is It Natural to Grow Old?

There are many limiting beliefs about aging and I believe the most dangerous one is the belief that "it is natural to grow old".

I agree we have to grow old, however I am recommending that we delay it to the very last minute.

> Delaying old age sounds sensible doesn't it? Just look at the ugly alternative we covered in chapter 3.

What isn't necessarily natural is to grow old at the rate deemed normal by your environment. Simply because everyone around you is growing older at a common rate does not mean you have to. Going with the flow is symptomatic of being a passenger on the Old Age Express. You sit back and let the train driver take you to the same stations as everyone else around you.

> You don't see your rate of aging as a problem, so you don't question it.

Death, taxes and growing old are all guaranteed events however like taxes, you can do things to maximize your years of living younger and minimize your elderly years.

There is no failure or no down side to giving it a go.

> To die is natural however to spend a third of your life in old age is un-natural. ...... Roselyn

**Retirement hails the start of old age**

Sadly, most people associate the beginning of old age with retirement, and for the past 120 years the accepted retirement age was 65. This is presently being pushed out by a few years in a number of western countries however, on the whole we have been raised to accept that retirement at 65 and it signals the start of old age.

The only advantage of retirment is
the time you have to
reset your inner clock
and claw back the last 10 years.

---

I believe the word retirement should be removed from the dictionary.

---

This retirement age has been around for over one hundred years and was based on economics and the mortality rates at that time. Doesn't it strike you as strange that it has taken over 120 years for our society to review this marker? What does life 120 years ago have to do with today? I should mention that the only reason the governments are reviewing it now is once again due to economics and mortality rates.

The funny thing about the retirement age 65 is that it was introduced by Prince Otto Von Bismarck and the German government in 1889. At that time life expectancy was 49 so the Prince set the retirement age to 65 with the expectation that no one will live long enough to collect their benefits.

# I Have Left My Run Too Late?

## Benefits of Experience

Some people are scared of reinvention or change because they believe they have to abandon everything prior to today, and start with a fresh piece of paper. It isn't so in this instance. One of the wonderful aspects to reframing your thinking about aging and resetting your inner clock is that you get a do over with hindsight and years of experience.

> You benefit from NOT starting with a blank sheet. You have years of experience that you didn't have the first time around.

Over the years you have accumulated contacts and information you didn't have before. More importantly you have experience and knowledge. Both of which are priceless. You may even know more about who you are and what is truly important to you. All you need now is time to capitalize on these great attributes. The true value of experience is when you get to use it in the future.

You must have some things that you wish you could do again with hindsight. What about things you have always wanted to do but work and life just kept getting in the way? What do you have to lose?

> You have the power to grant yourself the gift of years inserted into your life timeline today. You would do it for a loved one or a friend, so why not for yourself?

## It is Never Too Late

If you believe that you have left it too late to follow through on a dream, I strongly recommend that you take up the challenge and get back some of those valuable years. Work on reframing your beliefs about aging, reset your inner clock and give yourself the time to jump into that dream. While you are breathing you have a chance.

If you had another 10 years would you still believe that you had left your run too late to give it a go? There is no such thing as leaving it too late to reset your inner clock. Sometimes even a day makes a world of difference. How many times have you heard people say "if only I had one more day with ..."," if only I had taken a day off ..."?

> Regret is a poison that kills hope and joy. It taints all the great things you have accomplished throughout your life and why should it be the last thing you think about. I believe killing your regret before it kills you is a big enough WHY to get back those years.

Many famous people have achieved great things later in life. Don't believe that old cliché about old dogs and new tricks. Many wildly successful people found their success after their fiftieth birthday and they all have at least 2 things in common:

- success was achieved at a time in their life when society had written them off
- belief in themselves

The following is an extract from an article I came across on the CNN.com website. The article is titled "Famous Folks launched careers after 50" by Ethan Trex, Mental Floss - May 16, 2010.

It highlights some pretty famous people who did not become famous until they were in their 50's and older.

---

> Imagine getting to your 50's or 60's with the regret of not achieving your lifelong passion or getting this far and not having a dream left in you to follow. 'I might have been..." or "I'm too old to start over" is not in the realm of these famous people who created their greatest feats in their 50's, 60's and later in life. What if they had given up; we would not have their amazing contributions today. Here are Folks over 50 who have not only succeeded but prospered at a late age. .... Ethan Trex, Author May 16 2010

---

**Colonel Sanders** - Harland Sanders didn't become the fried chicken mogul until he was 65 years old.

**Taikichiro Mori** - He was an economics professor until he left academia at age 55 to become a real estate investor in 1959. Tokyo's real estate scene is at the heart of Mori's fortune. When he died in 1993, he was Forbes' two-time reigning world's richest man with a net worth of around $13 billion.

**Laura Ingalls Wilder** - Wilder's "Little House on the Prairie" is one of the world's most beloved children's books. She didn't publish her first novel until she was age 65, but she still managed to write one of the most beloved book and TV series of all time.

**Grandma Moses** - Anna Mary Robertson Moses, one of Americas best known artists, didn't start to paint until she was in her 80's. When her arthritis grew too painful to embroider, she decided to give painting a try in the mid-1930s. She was age 76 when she painted her first canvas. She painted for another 25 years; long enough to see the canvases she had sold for $3.00 fetch prices of more than $10,000 each.

**Stan Lee** – Creator of Spider-Man was age 43 when he began drawing superheroes. He didn't achieve international fame until 20 years later when Hollywood came knocking, and recently passed away in 2018 at the age of 95.

**Julia Child** – The famous TV Cook and show host didn't start her show until she was age 50. She only learned to cook at all, in her early 40's.

**Ronald Reagan** - Reagan had been an actor for a long time, but he wasn't elected Governor of California until he was age 55. He went on to become President of the USA, with a two-term run at it.

All of these now famous people re-invented themselves at one time or another. They did not give up.

## Find Inspiration in Others

Detailed information about the following amazing people can be found on the Internet. It is worth your while to ask Google for a list of all the people who have achieved success after they turned age 50. You will be wonderfully surprised.

**Harry Bernstein** – Author of The Invisible Wall: A Love Story That Broke Barriers. Harry started writing the book when he was age 93 and published when he was age 96. The story recounts his childhood struggles during World War I.

**Gladys Burrill** – Gladys ran her first marathon when she was age 86. She was recognized by the Guinness World Records and Hawaii House of Representatives after completing the Honolulu Marathon the age of 92.

**Peter Roget** – Peter retired from professional life by age 61. However, he suffered from depression and as a coping mechanism he started pursuing one of the things he really enjoyed doing—**making lists**. He devoted his time to creating a catalog of words organized by their meanings, and at age 73 he published his project under the title *"Roget's Thesaurus of English Words and Phrases"*.

**Kathryn Joosten** – Kathryn started acting at age 53 when she was hired as a street performer in Disney World. Seven years later at age 60, she became famous for her role as a personal secretary in the show *West Wing*. She also won her first Emmy Award at age 66 for starring in *Desperate Housewives*.

## Environmental Brain Washing

We are conditioned to accept our fate and there are even some of us who eagerly look forward to retirement. We get fed lies all our life about who we are, where we should go and what we should do. We are conditioned to follow the rules and norms of our society. We are so busy with the daily grind that we rarely question what we are doing and where our lives are going.

Everyday lies and stereotypical references on aging seep into our subconscious with devastating impact on our lives. They feed the PAV – your premature aging virus – every minute or every day.

> Your views on aging affect your everyday decision making too and that is why it is so important to re-frame your state of mind on aging.

### Corporations

The majority of us are unknowingly racing to and through old age faster than we need to be because it suits large corporations, governments and our social community who define and control the race. It suits all sorts of people for us to believe that we're aging fast. We don't need to be in the workforce; we should follow the rules; we shouldn't exercise too hard; we shouldn't do this or we shouldn't do that. The corporate world wants us to fit into their marketing niches so they can predict our spending patterns and reach their sales targets.

Insurance companies run on mortality tables which predict when we will die based on our gender, age next birthday, and propensity to smoke. It suits these companies for us to believe we are elderly when we fall into their preferred age bracket for old age. This makes it easier for them to develop products for the elderly and create advertising campaigns appealing to our aging subconscious. Their mortality tables have a sound statistical basis however not everyone is a statistic. You don't have to fit into their categories and age according to their self-fulfilling death tables.

### The Media

The media very rarely use people older than 35 in their campaigns, and when they do it is to advertise reverse mortgages or burial insurance. You are happily watching your favorite show when suddenly an advertisement shows you a nice silver-haired couple sipping cocoa reminding you to pick up the phone and buy your burial insurance before it is too late.

**Younger Generations**

The younger population expects us to be totally ignorant when it comes to technology. Granted, we may not have all the latest technology down pat, but we are not stupid. The assumption that once you reach a certain age you are useless and have to be treated as a juvenile is insulting. This is societies collective opinion, not fact. I don't know when it all started, but it's not a valid assessment of Baby Boomers or anyone for that matter.

We have all lived meaningful lives, tried many things, enjoyed success, made mistakes and experienced life. We have built things and worked with people from all corners of the world. Even people who have become completely homeless have valid experiences to share. You have a valuable contribution to make to your community and the people around you. Don't let them marginalize you!

I firmly believe that someone who is in their sixth, seventh or eighth decade on this planet has a lot more to offer than baby-sitting.

In past centuries, tribal elders were revered, because they had learned the hard lessons and the younger members of the tribe knew they would benefit from their experience. They survived hard times and they were able to pass these lessons on to the younger people in the tribe in the hope that they would advance further, faster and more safely.  Sounds like a smart tradition doesn't it?  Just because we have technology leading the way does not mean that your experience and human point of view is invalid and irrelevant.

STOP and think for yourself. STOP doing what people and the media are telling you to say, do and think. START doing and thinking for yourself. Take back control of your life.

*It is now or never and it has not been any more vital than NOW.*

## The Future Doesn't Belong to Just the Young

How many times have you heard, "The future belongs to the young"?

Due to our upbringing and the influence of our parents, friends, environment and the media, we are constantly being told that the world belongs to the younger generation. We have been brain washed into believing that once you reach the chronological age of 35, you are on your way out and it is all downhill from there. This is another myth that feeds the PAV.

This may have been true for previous generations but the world has changed. Our natural life expectancy is growing every year and our quality of life is improving every day. Science is continuously working on ways to improve the physiology of our bodies so we may live longer.

Most people think technology is one of the main reasons that the future belongs to the young, however technology is also a great tool that we can use to fight the good fight and coupled with our life experience we can join the designers of the future.

It has everything to do with you believing in yourself and that your life is worth living.

## Do You Believe that You are Too Sick to Change Now?

If you are dramatically out of shape or suffering from a severe illness and believe that you are physically and mentally not up to the challenge of changing, I ask you to give yourself a break just for a few minutes.

Changing your beliefs takes time. Persistence and intention are the two key ingredients. It doesn't happen over-night, except in unusual cases like mine, when I went from believing I was going to die in a few years to extending my life by seventy years.

A great starting position is to allocate a time of day when you close your eyes and dream a little. Dream about what your life will be like if you were to overcome even a little of the debilitating effects of your illness or tiredness. Dream about not giving in and fighting just another hour or another day. Just maybe you will start a new thought cycle and eventually make some of those minor adjustments you dream about. Think of how great it will feel to have five or ten minutes of your life back.

Start small and travel at your own pace but move it. Ultimately, it is your choice to fight every day or surrender. My vote is to fight and give yourself a chance. Go as hard or slow as you wish with lots of rest intervals to regain your physical and mental strength. It is mainly your state of mind that needs your help and you don't even need to get off your butt to work on this.

You may be thinking that it is easy for me to say this, but the truth is we are talking about your life, and it is worth making an effort. Your kids and grandkids will be inspired by you and love you even more. Just think of the great example you are giving them. Many war veterans and cancer victims have performed outstanding things because they never gave up.

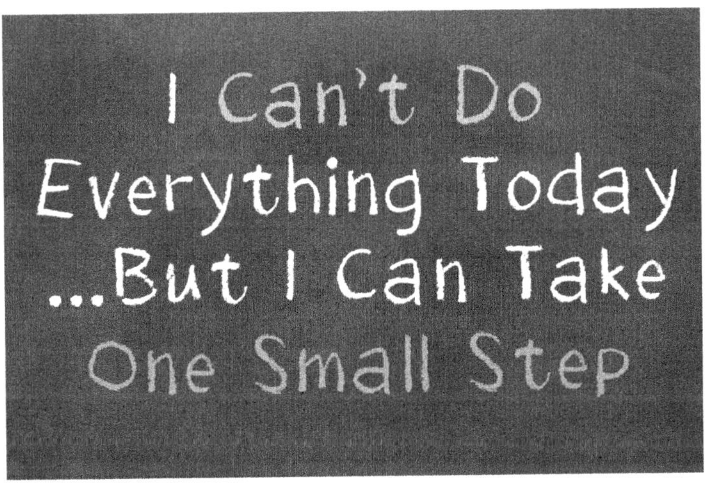

## Dreams Cost Money and I Have None

If you are like most of us and still working on your first million dollars don't lose heart.

If you are short on cash try scaling your dreams down a little, and scaling up your beliefs on resetting your inner clock to give you the time you need to regroup.

When time is on your side make the most of it. If you are chronologically 60, you have another 40 - 60 years to go. Look for solutions that you have never considered before. You have time for a second career; time to go to university, time to pay off a loan, time to reinvent yourself. All of this comes when you believe that you are younger than your birth certificate says, and you concentrate on using your younger mindset to learn new skills.

Remember training your state of mind to give you 10 – 20 years of living younger does not cost money. It comes from your own spirit to live.

Your mind is your personal Fountain of Youth.

## Ageism – Prejudice Against Age

Ageism like racism, sexism, and the other isms involves a negative pre-judgement based on an established and generally accepted "defined norm" or standard of what is right.

> Ageism is rife when it comes to employment.

People born in the 40's, 50's and 60's have decades of experience in all manner of subjects, including life. However, they are often ignored by companies who consider that they are out of date and too old to train. This is in spite of the fact that corporate is desperate for experienced personnel.

> "We need more experienced people in all industries because we can't afford to make business mistakes." ...Corporate Mantra

Employers believe older employees come with a lot of costly baggage:

- they are not up with the latest technology
  - older people don't understand the latest jargon
  - older people are out of touch with today's business processes
  - older people don't understand the way we communicate these days
  - older people don't understand the importance of the new ways of marketing and sales via social media
- their point of view is out of date
  - they don't relate to the younger consumers
  - our consumers won't relate to the old folks
  - older people won't work well with the younger staff members
  - older people won't like being told what to do by someone younger than them
  - management don't feel comfortable giving orders to someone who reminds them of their parents
- older people are an encumbrance
  - older people will take too long to learn the ropes
  - older people are not motivated
  - older people are not ideas people
  - older people move slower
  - older people think slower
  - older people will take more sick days

Do you believe any of these characteristics apply to you?

Personally, I believe that any of these characteristics can apply to anyone of any age.

We know that nothing beats experience, but sadly it is inexperienced people who are doing the hiring.

It is not going to be easy fighting against ageism but the first step is for you to refuse to buy in on it. Revalue yourself and appreciate your years of experience even if the HR departments don't. It is your life and you need to keep your eye on the truth and not what other people perceive to be the truth. It's a bit like Fake News; just because someone in the media or a blog says this or that, does not make it true.

## Technology has changed the Language not the Facts

Don't believe the world has left you behind because of technology. Technology is just a language that can be learned. I know this, because I have been an active member of the technology sector for five decades.

These days I am commissioned by large corporations to fix multi-million-dollar IT projects that have gone off the rails. The projects are in trouble primarily because the business people, who are usually a little bit older than the IT people, have been intimidated by the IT people, and left the decision making up to them. The business has wrongly assumed that the IT people know everything because they are in the forefront of technology. Wrong! The point is that the only thing they know is how to use the latest tools. They don't necessarily understand the business or the problems corporate face on a daily basis. In the majority of cases, they are IT specialists with very little experience in the real world of business. Their technical skill set does not make them smarter than you or I. They just have more up-to-date skill sets. It's a matter of respecting ourselves and our experience and doing something about bringing our computer skills and jargon up to date. Google is a brilliant source of support and help in this area.

Quite often we are intimidated by the new technology, but I frequently found that the abbreviations, jargon and terminology are in fact the only things that are new. The fundamental ideas and requirements of a lot of the software and technology we use today was highlighted years ago. It's simply that the new generation has given everything a new name or acronym. When it comes to design, business principals, and marketing principals, essentially, every generation seems to rename things just to confuse the previous generation. They operate as if it's something brand new, but quite often it's not. You just need to learn the acronyms and the new names that have been given to all these things. Once you get that, you'll have the key to what's actually happening.

Embrace technology rather than fear it. Surprisingly, technology makes it easier than ever for people of any age to learn whatever they want at their own pace, and in the privacy of their own home. Even the youth of today had to learn how to use the latest technology. It has nothing to do with age or when you start. One of the best tools that you could use, which I use every single day, is "Google".

Example: I just finished reading a financial paper that someone gave me to evaluate; I'm an Australian in America. It's all about the American Medicare financial problems; you know, retirement planning and pension benefits and things like this. The document was completely riddled with acronyms, so I couldn't understand a word on the first page. Every time I came across an acronym or a term I did not easily understand, I typed it in to Google to find the meaning. What is ABCD? Thank goodness for Google and the wonderful person who took the time to key in the definition or explain the process. Within minutes, I had educated myself in the acronyms used in the document. Once I translated the document, I was able to understand it and could contribute immediately to the discussion. Note, I said translated it.

It is all in the translation from cyber speak to human speak.

Don't buy into the belief that you're over the hill. All you need to do is smarten up a little and start to use some of these new technological tools. Remember when the fax machine and the first cell phones were introduced? This is no different and more importantly, you are no different.

One of the worst insults is when you are having some difficulty with your computer and someone tells you to ask your grandchildren for help. You might have been a captain of industry, a celebrated sports person or school teacher. Who knows? All of a sudden, you've got to find a ten-year-old to help you do something on your laptop or mobile phone. It is natural to feel deficient in this instance, however this is not reality. Everyone has to learn to do new things in the beginning. Even your ten-year-old had to learn from someone or somewhere. You are simply learning something new. Unfortunately, when these instances accumulate it can become overwhelming and you start to believe the whole lie that it's too late and you are over the hill.

Once you understand the language, then the tools, you won't have to ask a ten-year-old to help you. Simply, go to your PC and ask Google which by the way is non-judgmental.

The latest tools and technology can be taught, but there is no school for real experience in the real world other than doing it. Human experience is extremely valuable and those in power are confusing the value of experience with the ability to use the latest technological tools.

> Human experience is something that technology has great difficulty in emulating and you have decades of it... Roselyn

## Old Does Not Equal Brain Dead

One of the most toxic beliefs about aging is that older people have run out of ideas. This is backed up by another toxic belief that creativity is the realm of the young.

Unfortunately, these beliefs feed the Premature Aging Virus and further confirm the general belief that aging and irrelevance are one and the same.

We live in a society where these beliefs are considered normal and once again, we accept it because everyone around us is schlepping through the same swamp. We hear our friends complaining about the same things so it must be the status quo. Anyway, it is snug and comfy in our seat on the Old Age Express so why should we stir things up?

How many people do you know believe that once you hit age 40 getting a new job is just about impossible? Have you personally been on the receiving end of rejection simply because you were categorized as too old? How many times have you not applied for a position or project because you believed that you didn't have a snow ball's chance in hell of getting it because of your age?

Sadly, I know too many incredibly talented hard-working people who these days genuinely believe they are irrelevant in today's society, and seriously doubt their abilities. These toxic beliefs are propagated by pop culture and ignorant employers who believe the popular press without question.

Do you believe you are less intelligent than you were ten or twenty years ago? If you do, it is symptomatic of the Premature Aging Virus. Unless you are suffering from a brain related illness which has been medically diagnosed as the cause of your brain fog, it is more likely that you have accumulated more intellectual capital over the years and hence, smarter and more capable than ever.

We believe that we are over the hill and the younger generations believe they know everything. Sounds like a crazy co-dependent relationship to me, and we all know that this type of relationship is not good for either party.

I read a brilliant working paper recently which should go a long way to convincing you to replace your self-doubt with a well-deserved dose of self-confidence. The following was extracted from the 2018 paper titled "Age and High-Growth Entrepreneurship" authored by Pierre Azoulay MIT Sloan School of Management, Benjamin Jones Northwestern University, J. Daniel Kim Massachusetts Institute of Technology, and Javier Miranda U.S. Bureau of the Census. © 2018

> Our primary finding is that successful entrepreneurs are middle-aged, not young. The mean founder age for the 1 in 1,000 fastest growing new ventures is 45.0. The findings are broadly similar when considering high- technology sectors, entrepreneurial hubs, and successful firm exits. Prior experience in the specific industry predicts much greater rates of entrepreneurial success. These findings strongly reject common hypotheses that emphasize youth as a key trait of successful entrepreneurs. .....................
>
> Older entrepreneurs might access greater human capital, social capital, or financial capital. Taking a human capital perspective, younger people may lack experience in running companies, including the effective management of operations, marketing/sales, finance, human resources, and culture, or lack sector-specific knowledge regarding customer needs, regulatory constraints, or strategic opportunities – forms of "market knowledge" that may be important to successful innovation (Kline and Rosenberg 1986). In deeper technological areas, young people may not have sufficient scientific

knowledge to produce or manage effective R&D (e.g., Jones 2010).

Yes, it's a new world but the world is always in a state of constant change. Change is not new. You didn't have problems in the past keeping up, so suck it up and get on with it! All you have to do is believe in yourself and learn the new language of your culture and technology.

Personally, I've found that the best outcome for business and people is when we combine those who are experienced in life and business with those who use the latest tools. It makes sense. We do what we are best at and together we both learn.

The old adage -- you can't teach an old dog new tricks might apply to dogs, but you are not an old dog. You are a Life Olympian! ..... Roselyn

## Environmental Stereotyping Feeds the PAV

The Premature Aging Virus has been with you all of your life and it has made sure that you age in accordance with your fellow passengers on the Old Age Express. If you lived in a community where the majority of people lived to age 50, you would plan your life expecting to pass on around your fiftieth birthday. You wouldn't question it because it is considered normal. The same thing would apply if you lived in a community where people lived well into their nineties and beyond. Your life plan would be based on a minimum of ninety years.

---

Normal does not make it true or right.... Roselyn

---

The PAV and hundreds of subtle influences in our everyday lives, e.g. topics of conversation, how we refer to ourselves, advertising, just talking to your neighbor, things you hear in the news etc. all cover up the fact that aging is personal and in your control.

We buy into all of the pop culture beliefs that at retirement, we're too old to contribute to society, too old to be useful, too old to learn, too old to work, and no longer relevant.

The point is that you have the power to age at your own rate, and get back some valuable years. Your psychological age is under your control so use it. Reframe your beliefs about aging and find ways every day to reinforce your new living younger longer beliefs.

---

Grab the remote and change the channel.

---

**Be mind-full and question what is considered normal when it comes to aging, old age and time. You are unique and this is your life so have a go!**

## Medical and Bioscience Update

You know you can live younger longer than society dictates because you are now consciously aware that your mind and psychological age is your determinant. However, it is important to know that you are not alone in this fight to reset your inner clock, and get more out of life. The medical, scientific and biomedical engineering communities are focused on developing ways to extend our disease-free years, and ensure that we live a long and healthy life.

The following is a quote from a paper written by TBL Kirkwood, University of Copenhagen Center for Healthy Aging, Department of Cellular and Molecular Medicine, Copenhagen, Denmark, Newcastle University Institute for Ageing, Campus for Ageing and Vitality, Newcastle upon Tyne, UK.

---

"We are reaching old age in generally better health, and it is the death rates at advanced ages that are now falling fast. At the same time, biology has established that there is almost certainly no fixed programme for ageing, which is caused instead by the lifelong accumulation of damage. It is becoming evident that the ageing process is much more malleable than we used to think. "

We are living longer than our parents and the scientific and biomedicine sectors are working on extending not just our life but our health span.

The following is a list of just a few of the factors contributing to our extended mortality:

- Better medicine – life extending drugs like the ones that lower cholesterol and others that prevent cardiovascular disease.

- Improved medical practices – early warning screening for breast cancer and other cancers, surgeons aided by robotics and your local GP has ready access to global medicine research from his surgery.

- Advances in technology – faster telecommunications across the global medical arena, extensive ability to analyze big data on subjects like genetic sequencing, and 3D bioprinting.

- Biomedical Engineering also referred to as BioMed or BME is a multidisciplinary STEM field that combines biology and engineering. The research applies engineering principals and materials to medicine and healthcare.

- Research data – technology allows researchers from all over the world to collaborate much faster than any other time in history.

- Public awareness – electronic media delivers information educating us on how to care for ourselves and what symptoms we should be on the lookout for. A hermit living in a cave with internet connection can be as up to date as a millionaire living in the center of London. We are making smarter choices. Obesity is still a massive problem but smoking has declined from 45% 1965 to 15% in 2015.

- Processed foods – governments have enforced packaging rules on manufacturers and promoted public awareness of saturated fats and high fructose corn syrup.

Reframe your thinking about aging, reset your inner clock and be in the best possible position to benefit from what science and life have to offer?

## Life Expectancy

Time to die, according to who?

Reframing your beliefs about time, aging and old age could also result in extending your overall life span. I have included this section on life expectancy to help you realize that you have a few years left and it is not too late to reframe your thinking and reset your inner clock. People are living longer. I want you to live younger for longer.

Popular scientific opinion is that we are currently capable of living to age 120. However, in spite of this great news, most of us are still retiring at age 65, consider ourselves old at age 70 and on the way out by age 80. We are cheating ourselves of 20, 30 even 40 years of life by our outdated beliefs regarding our life time line.

Do not let the past rob you of your future... Roselyn

The generalization that most people pass away by the time they're in their 80's is an outdated belief. We are conditioned to think this applies to all of us. It only applies if you believe it and I for one don't agree. I'm going to be around until I'm 120 years of age. That's my belief. That's my race. That's what I am doing!

I can't guarantee that I will make it to age 120 but I will die trying... Roselyn

How long do you believe you will live? If, for whatever reason you believe that you will live to age 80, the chances are that it will become a self-fulfilling prophecy. Sure enough, at age 80, plus or minus a couple of years, you will be calling it a day. The wonderful thing about self-fulfilling prophecies is that you can use them to your advantage.

Why not create a self-fulfilling prophecy that sees you living a great life and celebrating your 120th birthday?

Why not use this time to see life as a series of experiences and do what you want to do? Life doesn't have to be all about a single major success or goal. It's your personal decision. Focus on keeping your big enough why alive. By keeping this mindset and living accordingly, there is a great chance that you will live a longer and younger life.

---

BTW: The world was home to nearly half a million centenarians (people ages 100 and older) in 2015, more than four times as many as in 1990, according to United Nations estimates. And this growth is expected to accelerate: Projections suggest there will be 3.7 million centenarians across the globe in 2050. ......Renee Stepler article World's centenarian population projected to grow eightfold by 2050, www.pewsearch.org

---

Enlightened people around the world no longer consider age 60 to herald the start of old age. It is just another point in time. What is your life expectancy, bearing in mind that life span is influenced by both your biological age and psychological age? Remember empowering beliefs about youth and aging are vital in your successful race for a younger lifespan.

USA has the second highest percentage of deaths caused by Alzheimer's and Dementia. A recent survey conducted by Becca Levy, Social and Behavioral Science Department, Yale School of Public Health, New Haven, Connecticut, United States of America noted that:

---

... participants who had a positive view on aging and old age reduced their risk of these types of diseases by 46%.

---

Longevity figures in America as of 2016 say that most men will live to 76 years old and women will live to 81 years old. The average is true, but you are not the average duck. If you genuinely believe you will live to 100 or even 120, your inner clock will re-set itself and your everyday decisions will subconsciously try to fulfill your prediction.

## Your Positive Age Beliefs Can Reduce Your Chances of Developing Dementia

> Positive age beliefs protect against dementia even among elders with high-risk APOE gene.
>
> Levy, BR - Social and Behavioral Science Department, Yale School of Public Health, New Haven, Connecticut, United States of America.

The following is an extract from a paper dated February 7, 2018 authored by a group of researchers claiming they have found positive age beliefs protect against dementia even among elders with the high-risk APOE gene.

Abstract:

One of the strongest risk factors for dementia is the e4 variant of the APOE gene. Yet, many who carry it never develop dementia. The current study examined for the first time whether positive age beliefs that are acquired from the culture may reduce the risk of developing dementia among older individuals, including those who are APOE e4 carriers. The cohort consisted of 4,765 Health and Retirement Study participants who were aged 60 or older and dementia-free at baseline.

As predicted, in the total sample those with positive age beliefs at baseline were significantly less likely to develop dementia, after adjusting for relevant covariates.

Among those with APOE e4, those with positive age beliefs were 49.8% less likely to develop dementia than those with negative age beliefs.

The results of this study suggest that positive age beliefs, which are modifiable and have been found to reduce stress, can act as a protective factor, even for older individuals at high risk of dementia.

Authors: Levy, BR - Social and Behavioral Science Department, Yale School of Public Health, New Haven, Connecticut, United States of America. Slade, MD - Department of Internal Medicine, Yale School of Medicine, New Haven, Connecticut, United States of America. Pietrzak, RH - Department of Psychiatry, Yale School of Medicine, New Haven, Connecticut, United States of America, and U.S. Department of Veterans Affairs National Center for Posttraumatic Stress Disorder, West Haven, Connecticut, United States of America. Ferrucci, L - Longitudinal Studies Section, National Institute on Aging, Baltimore, Maryland, United States of America.

Aging is a complex interaction of genetics, chemistry, physiology, and behavior. There is no downside and so many upsides to updating your beliefs on aging. There are hundreds of outdated beliefs and sadly we don't have the time to go through them all in this book. My objective here is to highlight the problem with outdated beliefs and inspire you to follow through on the exercises in this chapter.

> Psychologically, a lot of us think that we will probably age and die about the same time as our parents. Yes, that's right, whether we like it or not. If you accept that to be true like most things that you accept, it becomes a self-fulfilling prophesy.

The self-fulfilling prophesy idea is a pretty good idea, but you've got to have the right prophesy. I'm suggesting you change your prophesy today.

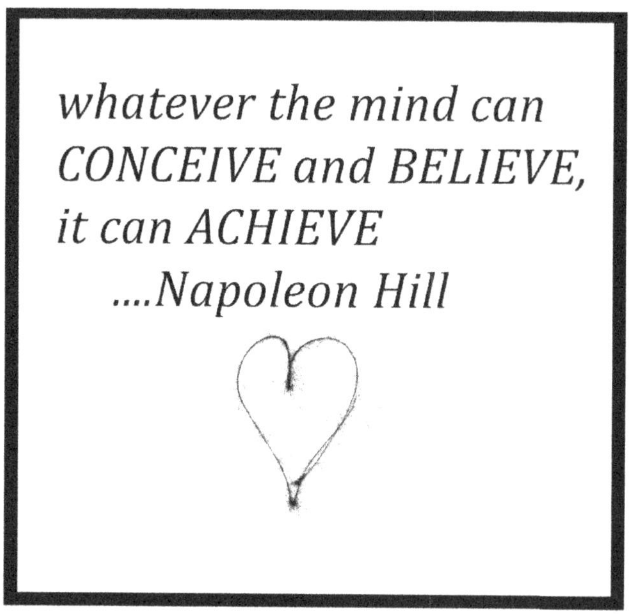

# Chapter 10

## Moving from Old to Bold

This is when the rubber meets the road. I have introduced you to the importance of your beliefs and the affect they have on your state of mind and habits, now we need to consciously apply what you have learned to your real world.

In brief, the road to reclaiming years of valuable life in your timeline involves:

- Awareness – aware that you are aging prematurely due to your environment, and that just because it is normal it is not necessarily right for you.
- Why – serious look at what old age means and the fabulous alternative available to you.
- How – the how is a multi-step process:
  - become consciously aware of your beliefs, state of mind and habits related to aging, and create a positive empowering set going forward
  - create a plan of change
  - implement your change plan

    - review your progress and check for congruency
    - keep going, don't stop
- When – now.

**AWARENESS** – by now you should be aware of the devastating affect your environment has on your rate of aging. If not, go back and read chapters 1 and 2.

**WHY** – the why is what motivates you and gets you through the difficult times. A big enough why will give you the will power and stamina to change and grow younger. Just looking at the alternative was a big enough why for me. If you need reminding read chapters 3 and 4.

## **HOW** – This is covered by the rest of this chapter.

## Step 1: Your State of Mind

Are you ready to change your thinking and subsequently your life moving forward? If you answered to no, please re-read chapters 3 and 4 for your own good.

You need to be in a state of mind that supports your passion to live younger longer. Be open minded and believe that you have the power to create your own personal Fountain of Youth. You have no chance of climbing a mountain if at first you don't have a deep enough desire to overcome the obstacles that you will encounter, and a core belief that you can do it.

Chapter 6 is dedicated to explaining states of mind and helping you to get a grip on your prevailing state of mind. It talks about the relationship between your beliefs, thoughts, environment and states of mind and being. I think the relationships sound a bit like the chicken or egg causality dilemma. Beliefs affect your state of mind and your state of mind affects your beliefs, infinitum. However, I am practical at heart so we have to start somewhere so for me you need to be in the most helpful state of mind to reclaim lost years. Jump in and believe. Allow the process to affirm your beliefs and in the meantime, enjoy the adventure. Like I have said before, what do you have to lose?

If you need some help invoking the right state of mind, I suggest reading Chapter 6 again and get your 'living younger longer' state of mind clearly defined and installed into your conscious mind ASAP.
Eventually your living younger longer state of mind will transition into your sub-conscious and be a part of your life's auto pilot program.

## Step 2: Install Your Younger Psychological Age

Decide on how old you feel or want to feel. Remember we are working with your psychological age not the age on your driver's license. At the start I reclaimed 13 years by resetting my inner clock from age 45 to age 32. Interestingly, 20 years later I have reclaimed a total of 21 years. I feel and function as a fit and happy 45-year-old, completely disregarding my driver's license age of 66. I have plans to grow my speaking and training career, build my Life Olympian social site, write another book, expand our Bunker Bradley Design business to include furniture, build a seaside home and artist studio on the coast of Australia and travel more. Just to name a few things.

Work on how to use your reclaimed years and start using them. Don't worry about justifying it or finding some amazing sound scientific basis for your ability. Just do it. This is your life.

## Step 3: Update Your Beliefs on Self and Aging

You can't change your circumstances until you change your thinking, and thinking comes from your beliefs. You can't expect to achieve a different outcome if your thoughts and actions remain as they always have. It is like wanting to drive to San Diego but you keep taking the route to Seattle because that is your usual destination. The Seattle route is in your sub-conscious and part of your auto pilot program. Your mind likes to do what is familiar. You need to become consciously aware of your beliefs, thoughts, habits and intentions if you are to reclaim years of younger life.

> By denying or ignoring the fact that you can control your premature aging, you deny yourself the ability to do anything about it.

**Beliefs About Yourself**

You can't change something if you don't know it exists, or knowing that it does exist you believe it can't be changed. In this instance we are talking about the Premature Aging Virus that robs years of valuable living from your timeline. You need to see and believe that you are aging prematurely, and that you are the one person who can do something about it. You have a vested interest in the quality of your life. Are you going to remain a passenger on the Old Age Express, or take responsibility and drive your own life from here on in?

The first belief that needs reviewing is your self-belief which includes your self-esteem and self-image.

Ask yourself if any of these apply to you bearing in mind each has an empowering opposite.

- I am not good enough
- I am not deserving
- I don't have what it takes
- I lack confidence
- I am not strong enough to swim against the tide
- I lack conviction and staying power
- I am too old
- I am set in my ways
- I can't imagine myself being different to how I am now
- I don't really have any control over my world or my life
- People and situations outside of my control always get in my way
- I can never escape my past
- Murphy's law always prevails.

I am not a clinical psychologist so I am not going to give you professional advice on how to deal with these mind-bending personal beliefs except to say, that each has an empowering opposite. Today there are many avenues available to you to get help with replacing these toxic self-beliefs with more empowering ones. Personally, I would start with identifying which self-beliefs I relate to and start researching on Google. Quite often Google will give you a few great clues as to what is going on and how to get in touch with people or groups who can help.

A real deal breaker is letting the past rob you of the future. Do you relive past failures repeatedly? When you contemplate a goal or an idea, just before your interest and enthusiasm takes hold, does your past come up and put the flame out with reminders of past failures? I am a great believer in that the only benefit of looking back is to take the lessons learned into the future so I don't repeat them again. Failure is ok if you stop crying in your soup and work out what actually happened and what you were supposed to learn from the experience.

Becoming consciously aware of your self-perception is key to any changes you want to make. If your personal core beliefs are not supportive of learning and change then your chances of success are severely limited.

Take time to work out what you believe about yourself and list the attributes that work in your favor and those that don't. Changing your core beliefs is like changing your persona. It is not easy and doesn't necessarily happen overnight. Concentrate on supportive attributes and beliefs and work out how to replace the negative ones. Every negative has a positive. You just have to find it, research it and implement changes to install the new belief. Take one step at a time. Like all change, it is best to take one thing at a time and work on it for 30 days, or until it feels natural to you. I was very fortunate to have a number of excellent race drivers take me under their wing and teach me how to race. One such driver was Alan Hamilton, a very famous Australian Porsche racing driver. The most important lesson he taught me was to concentrate on perfecting one corner at a time. A typical racetrack has over a dozen corners and it is difficult to think about one specific corner when all you want to do is get around the track in the least amount of time. However, he is right. Think about the one corner for the whole length of the track, plan your attack and execute it to the best of your ability. Accept the fact that you are human and it will take many approaches and slips before it becomes natural but keep focus. We can't focus on more than one thing at a time and hope to get somewhere.

Roselyn racing in Porsche Cup Series - Queensland

Look for reasons to believe that you are better off living younger longer than spending over a quarter of your life in old age. One of the great characteristics about beliefs is that once we believe in something, we sub-consciously seek reasons to support the belief.

Don't bother justifying why you used to believe this or that about old age and your age. We know why. It was the PAV thriving on your environment. You were aging on auto pilot, totally oblivious to what was happening to you.

---

> Behavior is the belief expressing itself and cannot be changed simply by changing your mind. What drives your behavior is not what you think but what you actually believe....
>
> Ray Dodd author The Power of Belief

---

**Changing Your beliefs About Aging**

Prior to my epiphany some of my views on aging were:

- It is inevitable
- I have no control over it
- When I was age 16, I could hardly wait to be age 18 to get my license (it is 18 in Australia)
- Oh no, age 30 is the end of the world as I know it
- Getting old is not going to be much fun
- Counting down the years – yes, I actually used to think about the number of years left on the assumption that the actuaries were correct and I was going to be old at age 65 and probably die at age 82.

Each one of these beliefs had an overwhelming influence on my feeling of wellbeing, my thoughts, views on the future, decision making and actions at the time, until my epiphany.

The minute I realized that I was a product of my environment and that it was not serving me I started my process of change.

---

> Expectations determine outcomes. If you expect your mental and physical capacity to diminish with age, it probably will. ......
> Deepak Chopra ... Grow Younger Live Longer

---

To effectively change your state of mind and subsequent future you need to work on your beliefs, habits and environment. All of these elements impact your state of mind and vice versa. Remember your environment affects your beliefs and they in turn affect your habits and state of mind and around we go. You need to develop new empowering living younger longer auto-pilot programs for your mind.

> You can't change your habits if you don't change the underlying beliefs that drive them.

Chapter 5 is about beliefs and one major characteristic of a belief is that it can change either consciously by you or sub-consciously by your environment. I am sure you can list many things you once believed in that no longer give credence to. Even beliefs that held great value to you can change over time. Change can occur due to any number of reasons, for example, a change in your environment, updated information, the belief no longer serves you, your emotional status changes, etc.

For example: There was a point in time when the majority of the people in the world believed the earth was flat. This theory held fast until a small group believed otherwise and eventually proved it to be round. This knowledge changed people's belief about their world and subsequently changed the decisions people made about their future.

> The issue is that over the years you have sub-consciously formed beliefs about your age, old age and aging in general, all of which contributed to the Premature Aging Virus that now need to be brought into the light of your conscious mind. You need to know what has been driving you so you can evaluate it and make the necessary changes.

Chapter 9 covers outdated toxic beliefs that can and do have an impact on your beliefs; however, this is not a conclusive list. It is designed to make you become aware of what is going on around you and to inspire you to research your influences and do something about them.

You can't change something if you don't know of its existence.

**How-To Systems Fail 95% of the Time**

There is a good chance that you have tried to change habits before and had varying degrees of success. The main reason for failure is that often we think all we have to do is change the action or the habit – simple. We don't delve into our sub-conscious and uncover the belief that is the root cause of the behavior or thought we want to change. Without understanding the underlying belief your change will be temporary. A bit like wallpapering over black mold, sooner or later the mold will become evident again. It is only after removing the mold before wall papering that you will have success.

Your core beliefs and subject related beliefs need to be in alignment and congruent. If there is even the tiniest misalignment your chances of success are doomed or at best short lived. Your actions reflect your beliefs and this is why "How-To" products fail 95+% of the time.

I want you to succeed and reclaim lost years of living younger which is why it is so important that you spring clean your mind and stock it with empowering valid up to date beliefs which will generate living younger longer habits and states of mind.

To live a healthier, richer, more creative life you need to recognize that most of what you hold to be true derives from habits of thought. We are born into a prevailing conversation about the world. As soon as we are capable of speaking, we engage in this conversation, reinforcing with our own thoughts and actions the patterns of thinking and behavior that surround us.... Deepak Chopra – Grow Younger Live Longer

**Knowledge is Power**

Know what you believe and test it in today's environment.

The first step in updating your beliefs is to work out which beliefs are working against you and those that are working for you. The quickest way to do this is to ask yourself questions about how you genuinely feel about your age and the future. Keep asking yourself questions. Your mind runs on auto pilot most of the time so it won't necessarily want to help you uncover all of its auto functions, but persist. Keep asking yourself questions and question the validity of your beliefs regarding old age, aging and your time in life. The world is constantly moving so some of your beliefs may not hold water now. Science, your environment, your situation all change over time so why not your beliefs? You will surprise yourself.

> You wouldn't think twice about helping a friend to extend their youthful years so why not help yourself.

Up to date information is one of the keys in changing your beliefs about aging. Your current beliefs have been with you for a long time and many of them are now outdated and simply irrelevant to your point in time.

As soon as you have written down your old beliefs you can start finding out about today's version of your beliefs. Personally, I have found the Internet to be an amazing help here, in that it is fast, economical, accessible 24/7 and has an overwhelming amount of information. If Google isn't your thing, I strongly suggest you take up the challenge and get in front of a computer and try it out. You will be amazed at how easy it is. Just type in your question and Google will overwhelm you with information.

You will be amazed at how the world has changed over the past 50 years. In fact, at times I have found the amount of new information overwhelming to the point where I have become bamboozled and exhausted just thinking about what I was thinking about. However, one of the great joys of this journey is that you are always learning new ways of doing things and I have learnt a big lesson, which because you have been so kind as to buy my book, I will give to you free.

If you happen to be a mere mortal like me, rather than go down the same track I did, try being a bit smarter. Take your time and look up one topic or belief at a time. You are no longer on that high-speed train to old age; you are sitting on the roadside in the sunshine reading your travel guides and mapping out your next adventure – this is your life and your time.

When you uncover some great new information write it down under a column headed TODAYS BELIEFS. Even if you find some information about aging and old age that you did not even have an old thought about write it down because it helps to bring you into this century. Remember we know a lot more today than we did last century, last year or even last week.

Finally, this is not a work sheet to be completed and filed in the bottom draw or left by the bedside. This is not a once only activity. This is about you and your beliefs, your world, your future. This is your new life coach, the source of your enthusiasm and your support mechanism, your friend, keep it with you and work with it daily.

---

> Remember, no matter how great your attitude is if you don't put in the work it means nothing. The magic happens when you get moving.

---

To live younger longer and reap the rewards now and in the future, you need to review and refresh your thinking and beliefs based on what is happening now, and continue to do so into the future. You have become consciously aware of your surroundings and you need to stay on top of it.

---

> Personal story: I used to think that reaching age 100 was a rarity, so rare in fact that in Australia, the Queen of Great Britain who is also the Queen of Australia, would take time out of her day to send you a personal telegram on your 100th birthday. This act alone confirmed my old belief that only a microscopic number of people reached age 100. I have since discovered that getting to 100 is now an everyday event. In the USA alone, there are currently over 100,000 centenarians, and the growth rate of this sector is growing faster than many younger age groups. In 1960 there were only 32,000. This statistic alone changed my view on living longer because if 100,000 people were currently doing it and millions were going to be doing it, then the season is wide open for living longer and by definition, stronger and younger, and I am going to be one of them.

---

I want to know what is around the corner, to laugh more, to accumulate more experiences, I want to live younger longer. Join me, what have you got to lose?

**Resources to Help You Change**

Change is not easy for us humans which is why there are so many books and consultants with great ideas on how to help us change.

Over the years I have studied and applied:

- NLP – neuro linguistic programing – great for reprogramming your mind
- Kaizen – this is a system that requires you to change one tiny step at a time
- Neuroplasticity – rewiring the brain through new habits creating new neural pathways – great author is Dr Joe Dispenza
- Jack Canfield also has a number of great programs to help us change.
- Vision boards – not so helpful for me because I become numb to them after a couple of days.
- Self talk – I use this one big time – keeps me on track.

The point is that change is a specialist field and it is better for you to seek books and programs that specifically work on the process of change rather than me try to replicate what other great authors have already researched and documented.

**Commitment and Intention**

Your intention is to live younger longer and defer old age to the last possible moment. This is your life you are working on and this fact alone should be enough to keep you committed to the changes you need to implement; however, if not then you need to work on your why and make sure the grizzly alternative is black enough to give you no other option other than focus on living younger longer.

Remain mindful and proceed with intention.

> "Motivation is what gets you started. Habit is what keeps you going." – Jim Ryun – US Politician

You will experience obstacles along the way and there will be times when you slip a little. Obstacles can be worked through. Talking to others is a great way to start breaking through an obstacle. Action is another way. Giving in is not the answer. Keep reminding yourself that you are working on your life.

Seek out people who are already living the life you want to live.

To slip a little, and require a reset is to be human. Don't take it personally and don't write off the future just because you slipped. Reset immediately and have another go.

Motion promotes emotion – doing is when the magic happens.

# Step 4: Possible Consequences of Change

**Something to consider on your new journey**

The feeling of losing rapport with your old friends, your old environment and not fitting in is likely to occur at some point.
It is true that the amount of common ground you have with your friends, family and work colleagues will reduce. This is to be expected because yesterday you were together on the Old Age Express, and today you are traveling under your own steam going in a new direction, so it is to be expected that the scenery and experiences along the way will be different.

My best advice here is to accept the change, knowing that there is a whole new set of experiences, people to meet, places to go and mountains to climb. This does not mean that you have to lose or abandon your old friends. It simply means that there will be points of difference and you will develop additional new friends along the way.

> Feeling alienated from your old world is only a temporary discomfort.

Remember you are not starting with a clean sheet of paper, rather you have chosen to take a different direction going forward. All of the pages in your life up until now are still in your book, it is the future plot that has changed.

Personally, I experienced a progressive disassociation with my old self and my old journey. The aspects that concerned me most were physical appearance, personal presentation, sports, interests and relating to old friends. Early on there were times I found myself dressing for an occasion on auto-pilot, only to find that the end result which had been previously more than acceptable was no longer appropriate. I did not feel comfortable, but what would I feel comfortable in? This is a pretty big question which took time to resolve. Change takes time and patience. Don't fool yourself you are changing.

Relating to my closest girlfriends was and continues to be interesting. We are all independent business women with busy lives and our monthly dinners were the best way for us to keep in touch with each other. After my epiphany I noticed that I had less to say at our dinners, and less interested in the overall conversation. My girlfriends hadn't changed. They were progressing through life as planned and were quite comfortable with their lot in life.

Obviously, I was no longer on the Old Age Express and was travelling a different route. I was experiencing challenges and events they could not necessarily relate to so it made conversation and rapport a little difficult for a time. I was also moving through new territory for me, though I was much better equipped than the first time I travelled through my thirties.

Since then, I have successfully acclimated to my living younger longer mind set and life. These days I am able to step onto the Old Age Express and visit my old friends without feeling threatened of losing my position on my journey or falling into the old habits. I am fully aware of my surroundings which means these temporary environmental changes don't have any effect on my sub-conscious. My awareness filters out the toxic beliefs on aging and old age without me even thinking about it. My living younger longer mind is on auto-pilot. I can quite happily visit and listen to their stories and understand how they are going, knowing that this is just a visit, and I will get back to my own journey any minute. I admit that I am sensitive to their feelings and I try not to boast or be overly excited about my latest adventures. However, Facebook does give me away a little.

## OVER TO YOU

Be thankful for the fact that you are where you are and move forward from here. Believe you can reset your inner clock and get on and do it. Time and your mind will naturally re-enforce your belief.

> Get into your living younger state of mind and stick with it through thick and thin. Remember this is your life.

We are conditioned to fit in and you have been doing an exemplary job so far, so you know that you can do it, you just need to change to a living younger longer group. How about swapping your spectator crowd for the exciting do it now team?

Recognize and believe that your old state of mind and outdated beliefs of where you are in your time line are limiting your potential to have an even greater life ahead of you.

Remember you don't' have to become old or stay old. Replace your old outdated limiting beliefs with fresh up to date thoughts, feelings and actions that will activate your new beliefs. Supercharge your living younger state of mind.

Remind yourself daily why you are reframing your beliefs on aging, and add to it as often as possible. When in doubt look at your why and the alternative.

Believe in your core that are younger today than you were before you picked up this book and that you can live beyond the status quo of 85 years old.

Formulate an action plan to reinforce your new beliefs. This plan should incorporate your life time line (0-100 years on a line drawing) and the how-to *roadmap* (your action chart with many boxes showing what to do when...?)

You also need to plan "how to implement" your roadmap with advanced visualization, anticipating problems and changing directions to accomplish your new life's plan which allows you to live younger longer with gusto.

***Ready***

No Regrets
All is forgiven
Only the future lies ahead

Ahead
The race that I must run for fulfillment
The fibers of my body twitch with youthful strength
The drive and motivation of my passions pulsate my veins
Hope fills my heart
My power has returned
Full of life, peace, love.

Love of readiness
For challenges, opportunities
Ready to seek what is mine
Ready to attain

Share the accomplishment
Accomplish the dream that once lost
Alive for today, the moment
Alive for now and tomorrow
Alive and looking forward

*Jeff Manning*

from The Dream Builder by Jeff Manning

**The only thing left for me to say is: "stop reading, start doing and get on with the rest of your wonderful life".**

## About the Author – Roselyn Poon

The fifties and sixties were not the easiest times to be a young half Chinese half Australian girl in Melbourne, Australia. Every morning before school my mother would lovingly remind me that I was a second-class citizen, and that I had to work harder than everyone else so I wouldn't be looked down on by the other kids and teachers. Mum's daily mantra set me on the fast track to understanding people and why they say and do what they do. My study of the human race extended to adults when at the age of ten I started working nightly at my Chinese uncle's restaurant. Each night over a bowl of rice he would talk about life values and the importance of working hard and respecting our more experienced elders. This was a magical time and I believe this is when I first started to work out how to meld my youthful enthusiasm with older wisdom.

I learned early on that specializing in effective communication and cognitive behavior were my tickets to a fulfilling and exciting life. At seventeen I was a member of the first group of women in the Australian IT industry, and at the age of twenty-seven I founded the software company Computer Link. We specialized in designing and building systems that work with humans rather than against them. Technology afforded me many great opportunities for learning and growth including becoming Australia's first professional female Porsche racing driver with my own race team.

Being born into a working class multi-racial family taught me to work with what I was born with, because that was all I had. This led me to a lifelong quest of learning how to get more out of my brain which led me to become a qualified Neuro-Linguistic Programmer. Over the past couple of years, I have added Neuroplasticity to my studies and this has seriously supercharged my capacity to grow.

I know how hard it is to develop and move through the world when you have a basic belief that you are second class. My mission in life is to help others feel good about themselves and show them how to maintain a healthy self-esteem through to the end. As we get older it is harder to feel worthy and involved which is why I am on a massive Premature Aging Virus Awareness campaign.

It isn't that I don't want us to get old it is just that I don't want it to happen until the very last minute.

Made in the USA
Columbia, SC
02 July 2020

13010689R00117